Ginseng : its cultivation, harvesting, marketing and market value, with a short account of its history and botany

M G. 1868-1946 Kains

Nabu Public Domain Reprints:

You are holding a reproduction of an original work published before 1923 that is in the public domain in the United States of America, and possibly other countries. You may freely copy and distribute this work as no entity (individual or corporate) has a copyright on the body of the work. This book may contain prior copyright references, and library stamps (as most of these works were scanned from library copies). These have been scanned and retained as part of the historical artifact.

This book may have occasional imperfections such as missing or blurred pages, poor pictures, errant marks, etc. that were either part of the original artifact, or were introduced by the scanning process. We believe this work is culturally important, and despite the imperfections, have elected to bring it back into print as part of our continuing commitment to the preservation of printed works worldwide. We appreciate your understanding of the imperfections in the preservation process, and hope you enjoy this valuable book.

Ginseng

Its Cultivation, Harvesting, Marketing *and*
Market Value, with a Short
Account *of* Its
History *and*
Botany

By M. G. KAINS

NEW EDITION

Revised, Enlarged *and* Brought Down
to Date

Illustrated

New York
ORANGE JUDD COMPANY
1903

Copyright 1899
BY
ORANGE JUDD COMPANY

Copyright 1902
BY
ORANGE JUDD COMPANY

SB
295
G5
K13
1902a

In compliance with current
copyright law, LBS Archival
Products produced this
replacement volume on paper
that meets the ANSI Standard
Z39.48-1984 to replace the
irreparably deteriorated
original.

1990

PREFACE.

During recent years, the news has been spread far and wide by the press that the consumption of ginseng in China is enormous; that our native forest supply is rapidly decreasing; that the price paid by our dealers is steadily advancing; that the plant can be cultivated, and that there is a considerable margin of profit in growing it. As a result, the agricultural papers, the Experiment Stations and the Department of Agriculture have been besieged with questions bearing upon all phases of ginseng cultivation, and many useful articles in addition to three bulletins have been prepared upon the subject. But, since the former, in addition to being too brief to be more than outlines or introductions, are unavailable to the majority of would-be cultivators, and since the latter contain much that does not interest the novice, the writer has prepared the following pages to be used as a practical working manual in the growing of this crop.

In its preparation, use has been made of some of the articles contained in agricultural journals, the United States Consular Reports, the bulletins published by the Pennsylvania Department of Agriculture and the Experiment Station of Kentucky. But the author has relied mainly upon his report to the United States Department of Agriculture, which was prepared for the Division of Botany in the summer of 1897 and published as the revised edition of Bulletin No. 16 of that division, the original issue and its reprints having been exhausted.

In that pamphlet was contained all that was then known to be of value in the cultivation of ginseng, and it was favorably received by cultivators of this root throughout the land. In the present treatise, the experience gained by many growers during two more seasons of experiment and observation has been added and the book thus brought up to date.

The information here presented has, therefore, been gathered from many reliable sources and is thus really the work of several authors, for whom the writer has acted in the capacity of secretary. Among many to whom thanks for valuable assistance are due—a list too long to give each separate mention—special notice must be given to the Division of Botany, United States Department of Agriculture, the Pennsylvania Department of Agriculture, and the Experiment Station of Kentucky for the use of several illustrations throughout the book, and to Messrs. Samuel Wells and Co., Cincinnati, Ohio, for helpful letters concerning markets.

M. G. KAINS.

PREFACE
TO THE SECOND EDITION.

Since the appearance of the first edition of this book, which is now designated Part One, ginseng growing has made such rapid strides and the demand for information has increased so greatly that a second and extended edition has become necessary. The information contained in the present volume, which is nearly three times as large as the first, has been culled from a large mass of material and is deemed to be the best that has appeared since ginseng culture first attracted attention in America. As in the first edition, the author, who wishes to be considered merely a compiler, has endeavored to present the ideas and experience of others without forcing his own views upon the reader. It will be noticed, however, that he has stated his opinions upon certain points and has striven to make clear others that seemed to need explanation. He wishes hereby to thank all who have given him help, especially those whose names appear in the text. He also wishes to apologize to nearly a thousand readers who have been compelled to wait for the appearance of this book.

The particular attention of the would-be investor in ginseng culture is called to the section in Part Two on "Profits." A decline in price and a more healthy market seem to be assured, a consummation that will result in the abandonment of speculation and the establishment of ginseng growing in America upon a firm commercial instead of the present uncertain nursery basis. Accompanying and fostering this development, however, must be a rational application of energy to the industry, especially to the improvement of the root, which under present methods would be doomed to deterioration because the forced seed production, now occupying general attention, is at the expense of root development.

Finally, ginseng culture will grow in proportion to the application of intelligence to it. The grower should always strive to be bigger than his business, a fact which, simply because he is in it, seems to be evident. That is, the reason he is in it seems to prove him to be progressive and to keep himself abreast of the times. He should endeavor to maintain this state by reading and discussing all matters pertaining to farm life, because much that may appear to bear no apparent direct connection with ginseng, for instance improved marketing methods in general, will be found helpful in dealing with problems that arise in the business of growing and selling this root.

M. G. KAINS.

New York City, November, 1902.

CONTENTS.

History	1
Botany of the Plant	5, 55
Natural Home of the Plant	14
How to Begin	14, 58
Starting with Wild Roots	14
Starting with Seed	16
Climate and Location	18
Soil	19, 59
Preparation of the Beds	21
Preparation of Permanent Beds	25, 62
Planting the Seed	26
Treatment of Seedlings	28, 62
Treatment of Permanent Beds	30
Artificial Propagation	30, 65
Protection of Beds	31
Manuring	32, 65
Shades and Shading	33
Enemies	36, 66
Selection for Improvement	37, 69
Cultivated Versus Wild Root	40, 72
Preparation for Market	41
Profits	46, 77
Clarification	75
Adulteration and Fraud	88
The Asiatic Ginseng Industry and Market	94
Letters from Growers	106
Medicinal Properties	130
Protection by Law	136

LIST OF ILLUSTRATIONS.

Fig.		Page
1.	Human Form of Root	2
2.	American Ginseng Plant	4
3.	Yearling Plant and Two-Year-Old Root	6
4.	Stems, Leaves and Flower Cluster	7
5.	Fruit Cluster on Plant	11
6.	Three and Four-Year-Old Root	11
7.	Divisible Root	12
8.	Stanton's Forest Seed Bed	22
9.	Garden Plantation with Lattice Shed	24
10.	Weeding Horse	26
11.	Handy Marker	27
12.	Lath Screen for Shade	35
13.	Irregular Roots	38
14.	Dried Root	45
15.	Map Showing Natural Range	56
16.	Kelsey's Lath Shade	63
17.	Kelsey's Planting Board	64
18.	Korean Ginseng	108
19.	Parent's Ginseng Garden	112
20.	Nusbaum's Ginseng Garden	114
21.	Bates' Ginseng Garden (exterior)	119
22.	Bates' Ginseng Garden (interior)	122
23.	Kelsey's Ginseng Garden	124
24.	Hart's Ginseng Garden	137

PART ONE.

THE GINSENG INDUSTRY.

THE GINSENG INDUSTRY.

HISTORY.

In discussing the cultivation of a well-known crop, such as the apple, or the onion, an author need mention nothing as to its history. The great majority of readers are not interested in such matters, and will skip over to the more practical parts which deal with cultural directions, yield and profits. But in writing of a new crop, especially one that can never become a staple, it is necessary that the reader should know something of its development, in order to judge of its advancement and the probable limits of the market. He will then be in a good position to judge whether or not to start for himself. The following brief introductory paragraphs, therefore, are inserted to show the development of trade in American ginseng from its earliest stage to its present position of commercial importance.

Chinese ginseng, to which American ginseng is closely related, has been to the Chinese of vastly more importance than quinine has been to the nations of more progressive ideas. Unlike quinine, however, which is prescribed for a limited number of ailments, ginseng is considered a sovereign remedy for almost every malady that human flesh is heir to, from indigestion to consumption, and is believed to insure immunity from all kinds of disease. There is still a more remarkable belief in the properties of this plant. It is thought that certain specimens, like the one represented in Fig. 1, which bear a somewhat close resemblance to the human form, are specially useful in certain ailments. For instance, the leg-like parts are particularly valuable for leg troubles; the arm-like portions for affections of the arm, and so on. Whole roots of this form are believed to be capable of prolonging life itself, and are consequently very highly valued; in fact, cannot be purchased for less than their weight in gold. Truly, the plant is well named *panax*—a panacea. It is, however, not dependent wholly upon superstition for its power, but is possessed of medicinal qualities, more highly prized in it by the Chinese than by us, since we have a number of drugs that we use in preference. By us ginseng is recognized as possessing slightly stimulating and mildly aromatic qualities, as well as demulcent, alterative, carminative and tonic properties. It is probable that these were discovered by the Chinese before the qualities of more valuable drugs of the same class were discovered, and that the main reasons for its present popularity in China are the conservative ideas of the Chinese and their belief in supernatural affairs, which, coupled together, exalt the merits of the plant unduly. In America, the root is seldom used except as a demulcent, and even for this purpose we have other drugs that are more popular.

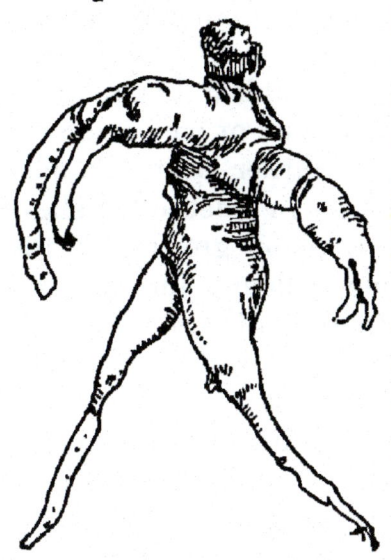

FIG 1. HUMAN FORM OF ROOT.

The reverence in which the plant is held, and the high price that it commands in the open markets of China, of course led to untiring search for a substitute, not only in adjoining countries, but in remote parts of the world. Roots were, and still are, found in Japan and Korea that so closely resemble ginseng in appearance that even experts find difficulty in detecting them when mixed with the true root. These roots, however, have no value, and are appreciated only by the unprincipled men who use them as adulterants of true ginseng, or as substitutes therefor.

Search in America, however, resulted more favorably. A plant (*Panax quinquefolium*), Fig. 2, was found that not only resembles the Chinese root (*P. ginseng*) in appearance, but possesses its medicinal qualities. In 1714 Father Jartoux, a missionary among the Chinese, published "A Description of a Tartarian Plant called Gin-seng" in the Philosophical Transactions of the Royal Society of London, a copy of which shortly afterward came under the eye of Father Lafitau, a missionary among the Iroquois Indians in Quebec. Believing that there might be such a plant growing in the Canadian forests, Lafitau made diligent inquiry and untiring search for it, and after about two years his efforts were successful. In 1716 the plant now known as American ginseng was found near Montreal.

Roots were gathered and dried by the Indians and sent to China, where they were so well received that a considerable trade in ginseng sprang up. The roots were purchased from the collectors at about thirty-five cents a pound, and were often sold in China for ten or twelve times that amount. At that time all the trading in this root was done by the officers and crew of a French trading organization, the "Company of the Indies." When, however, the directors of the company discovered that there was a wide margin of profit to be made upon this root, they assumed control of the industry and prohibited the private ventures of their employes. This move had a marked effect upon the price, which quickly rose to more than five dollars a pound. Good prices such as these might possibly have been maintained had

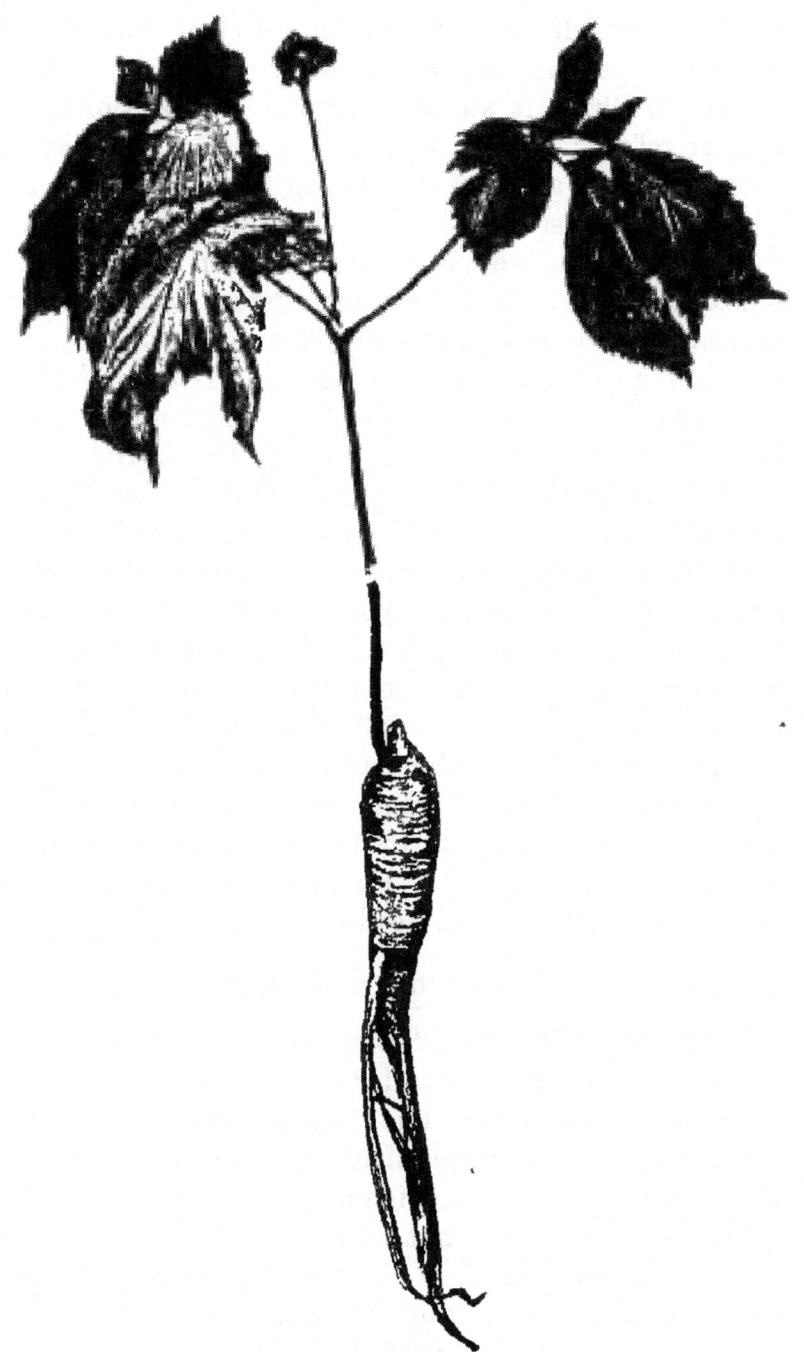

FIG. 2. AMERICAN GINSENG.

it not been for an excessive demand made in 1752, as a result of which an immense quantity of root was dug out of season and improperly dried in ovens. Upon its arrival in China it was found to be so inferior that the dealers refused to accept it. In a single year the trade dropped from about $100,000 to $6,500, and in a few years more ceased entirely. The Chinese faith in the Canadian article was so severely shaken that the standing of the American root also suffered, an effect that it has taken more than a century to overcome.

During these years, and particularly those following the event just recorded, the New England states, and later the sister states as far west as the borders of the Mississippi, profiting from the ill-luck of their northern neighbor, increased their trade until, in 1858, more than 350,000 pounds were exported, but at the low average figure of 52 cents a pound. Since that year the quantity of root exported has decreased, but the price has improved. In 1897 the price per pound reached its highest average, $4.71, slightly more than nine times the price in 1858. This steady increase is a hopeful sign that confidence is being restored, and forms one of the strongest arguments in favor of the cultivation of the root in this country. Further data upon this topic may be found under the heading, "Profits."

BOTANY OF THE PLANT.

American ginseng (*Panax quinquefolium*, L.) is a member of the natural order *Araliaceæ*, which is allied to the Parsley family. The plant, when old enough to bear seed, is easily recognized, and, especially when in fruit, is somewhat conspicuous; but during the first two or three years it is not particularly prominent. The seedlings appear, in New York state, about the first of May, sometimes a week or so earlier. They at first look something like newly sprouted beans, in having two

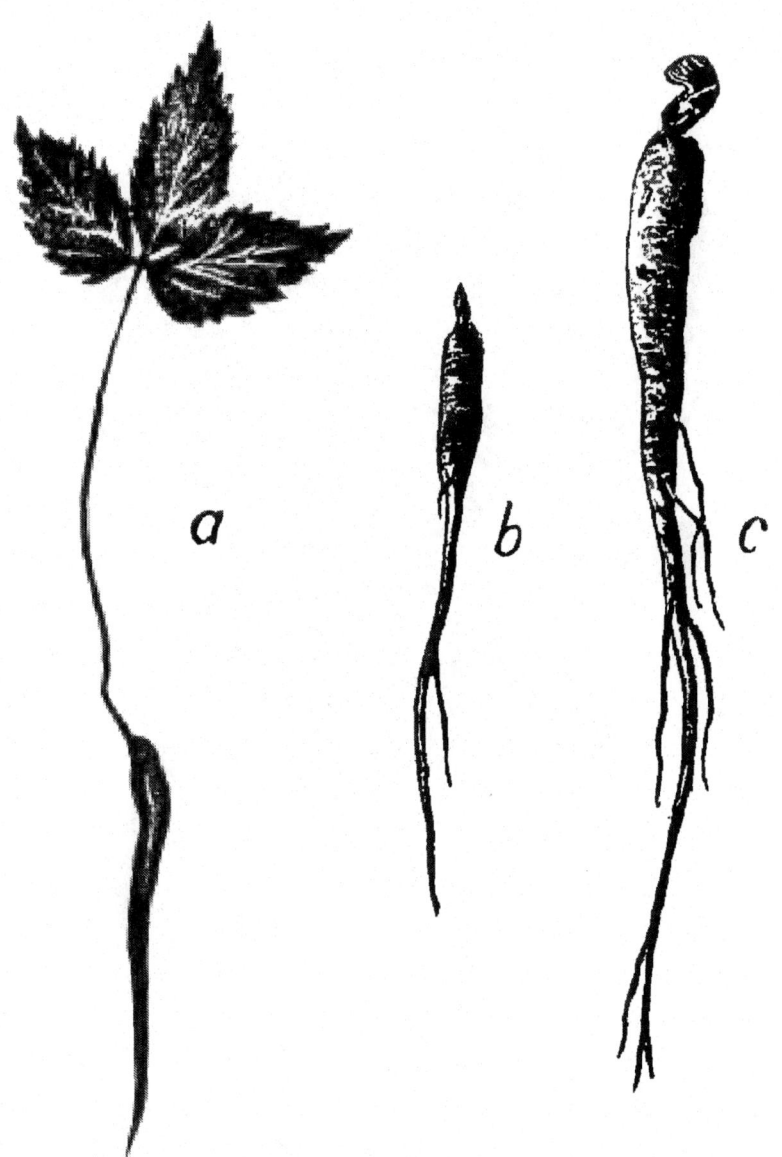

FIG. 3.
a, Yearling ginseng plant in July; b, yearling root in October; c, two-year-old root.

seed leaves (cotyledons), between which is a little stem and one, two or three tiny leaves. These are the only leaves borne by the plant the first year, and they seldom rise more than a couple of inches above the ground.

FIG. 4. STEM, LEAVES AND FLOWER CLUSTER.

They are usually fully developed in four or five weeks from the first appearance of the plant above ground, and this is true of older plants as well. Fig. 3, *a*, represents a yearling plant when full grown as it is seen in July, and *b*, a root as it appears in October. The whole work of the plant the first two, three, or even more, seasons, is to develop the solitary bud that is to produce the leaves and stem of the following year. This bud is borne at the crown of the root, and is called by the Chinese the "head." When growth ceases, the stem breaks off beside the bud, leaving a scar that is always retained. Fig. 3, *c*, shows the bud and the scar on a two-year-old root as it appears in October.

During the second year the plant may produce from one to three branch-like stems with from three to eight leaflets, and may reach a hight of five inches. In the third year from eight to fifteen leaflets may be produced, and the plant may grow eight inches tall. In after years there may be as many as four leafstalks, each bearing usually five leaflets—sometimes three or seven—arranged, as in the horse-chestnut leaf, like the fingers of the hand, as seen in Fig. 4.

The two smallest leaflets are an inch or two long, the others three or four. In outline they are egg-shaped, with a saw-toothed margin and an abrupt point. The large end is away from the stem. In cultivated beds specimens with five leafstalks and twenty-five or thirty leaves may be found, and they may reach a hight of thirty inches, though twenty is as tall as they usually get in the woods. The stems of mature plants are generally about the thickness of a lead pencil.

The flower stalk, which is usually from two to eight inches long, according to the strength of the plant, is borne erect at the point where the leafstalks branch out (Fig. 4), and bears in late June or in early July a cluster of inconspicuous, odorless yellowish-green flowers arranged in an umbel somewhat like the flowers of parsley or carrots. The fruit is soon formed, and develops from green in August to a handsome scarlet in the middle of September, when it reaches full maturity. The berries, which are edible, have the taste of the root, and are about the size of small wax beans (Fig. 5). They contain from one to three seeds, usually two. Seeds are produced by plants three years old and upward, though

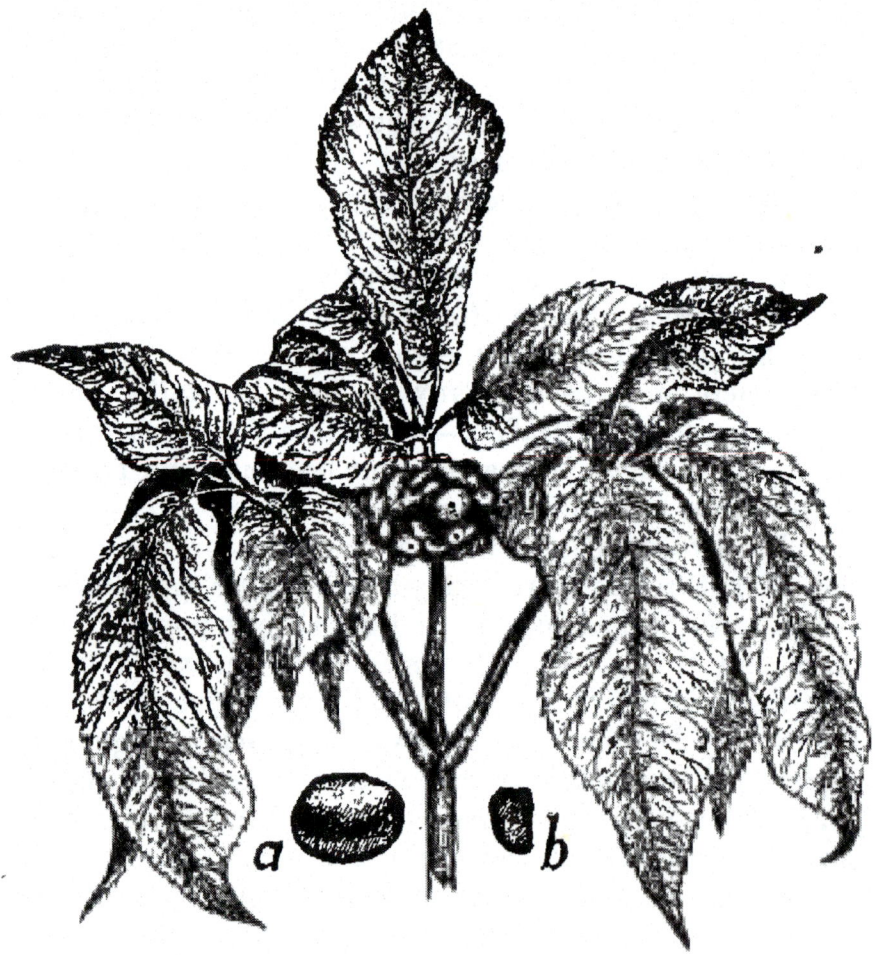

FIG. 5. FRUIT CLUSTER ON PLANT.
a, Berry; b, seed, natural size.

occasionally an unusually strong plant may produce seed the second year. In the cultivated plots the production of seed is generally much greater than in the forest, from forty to sixty being commonly found, though one hundred or more may often be borne upon a single head. Plants with several stems may have a cluster of fruit upon each stem, though these will usually be smaller than upon plants of the same age where only one stem appears. In the woods the plants seldom bear more than fifty seeds, and usually not more than half that many.

The root, which is the part of commercial importance, is composed of two parts—the rootstock and the root proper. The former, rarely more than one-third of an inch in diameter, shows the scars, already mentioned, each one of which indicates a year's growth. Specimens have occasionally been collected that were over fifty years old, and one has been found that has reached the age of sixty-five. Size and value do not, however, increase, but diminish with age after a certain stage in the development of the plant has been reached. The power of producing seed is also lost to a greater or less extent. The old specimen referred to was very much shriveled, weighed less than half an ounce, and was scarcely more than one-third of an inch thick.

As a general thing, when the roots have attained a certain age they gradually decrease in size and weight year by year, and at the same time lose their medicinal qualities. They continue to shrink until they become mere bundles of woody fibers, shadows of their former selves. They may, however, take new courage and send out new roots near the crowns, which, as the original roots become more and more feeble, gradually take their places and do their work. When this is accomplished the old roots die and slough off. This is not a form of reproduction, but of the continuation of the life of a single plant. Young roots may often reach a weight of two or three ounces after drying, and a diameter of one and a half inches. Some specimens have been gathered that weighed half a pound, but these

BOTANY OF THE PLANT.

are now rare, the constant search for the plants tending to prevent their full development. Such sizes and weights are, however, possible in cultivated beds.

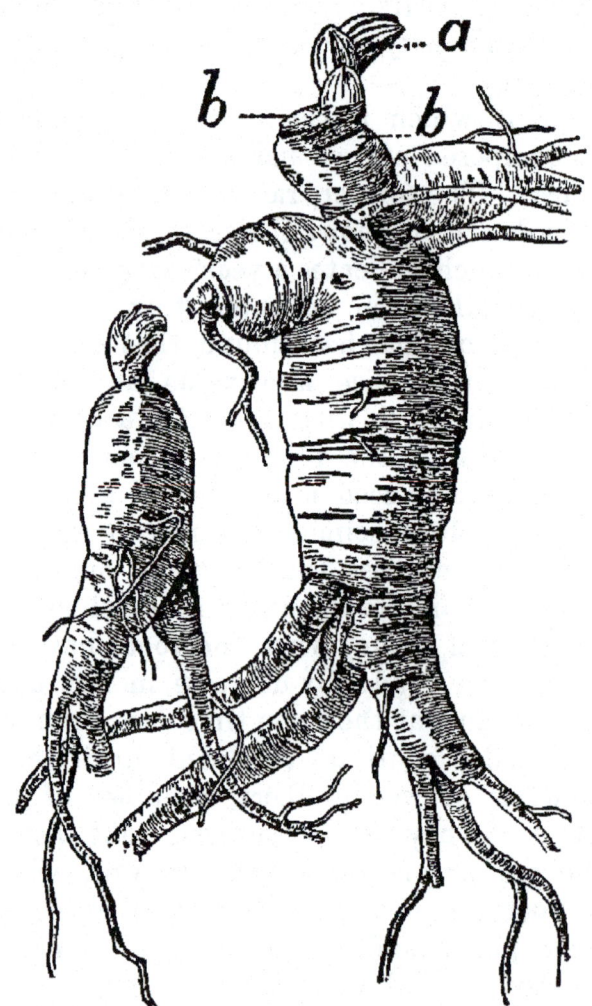

FIG. 6. THREE AND FOUR YEAR OLD ROOTS.
a, Bud; *b*, scar.

When young, the root is shaped and colored like a little parsnip, but usually becomes more or less forked and darker in color as it grows older. Its size is largely governed by the supply of food, exposure and other conditions influencing its growth. When one year old it is usually about an eighth of an inch in diameter, and about an inch when five or six; and after the first year or so, it is plainly marked with wrinkles running part, or even all, the way round it. Roots of three and four years of age are represented in Fig. 6.

Ginseng reproduces itself naturally by seed only. When cultivated, and occasionally even in the forest,

FIG. 7. DIVISIBLE ROOT.

plants may be found that bear from two to four stem roots, like the one shown in Fig. 7, which spring from near the base of the rootstock at the crown. These, if carefully removed, may be made to produce as good roots as if grown direct from seed. In this particular case three plants could be obtained from this one root. An advantage that they possess is that they will attain a marketable size and produce seed sooner than seedlings. It seems possible, too, that the rootstocks might be made to produce roots in the same manner as ordinary cuttings. This, so far as can be learned, has not yet been done.

From what has been said, it is clear that ginseng must not be dug in the summer, because if the roots be harvested before the seed is ripe the latter will be lost. In the forest this is actually taking place, and is the principal reason why the price of ginseng is rising year by year; the pasturing of stock in the woods and the destruction of the forests by widening agriculture or by fire being the only other important influences toward its extermination.

The dealers claim that they are still able to obtain the root in nearly the same quantity as formerly, but they say that it is coming from places more remote each year. The latter statement is certainly true, but a glance at the export figures, given under the heading, "Profits," will show that the former is probably overestimated, because the quantity sent abroad is decreasing year by year.

The principal agents in the extermination of the native supply are the ginseng hunters, "sang-diggers" they are called. They exercise no judgment whatever in collecting. They take even the tiniest roots whenever they see them, whether in April, June or November, and the plants are thus given no chance to reproduce themselves. It is of little consequence to these shiftless people to be arrested and jailed according to the laws of the two Virginias and of Ontario. They take the matter coolly and live at the expense of the state until the end of their sentence, and go back to dig as before. When the plant is cultivated it will be to the grower's interest to dig at the proper season, and to prevent, as much as possible, the digging of the wild root in his locality during the spring and summer.

There is, however, a more important reason for digging the root after the ripening of the seed. During the summer the plant is expending its energies in growth and the perfection of its seed. As a consequence, the root is in poor condition, and is thus unfit for the uses to which it is put. But in the fall, when the seed has been matured and the plant has stored food with which to commence the following year, the root is in its best condition, being not only firmer and heavier from the stored nutriment, and thus liable to less shrinkage in drying, but it is more valuable as a drug. A given weight of green roots will realize more when dug in season and properly dried than when gathered in the summer.

NATURAL HOME OF THE PLANT.

Ginseng may be found growing wild as far west as the first tier of states west of the Mississippi, and from Canada to the Gulf of Mexico. In the warm south, it confines itself to the mountains and other high ground where the temperature is relatively low; in the north, it descends to the low lands. It delights in the rich, moist, but well drained soil from which our oak, maple, beech and basswood forests spring, but not in the wet and muddy soils that support the tamarack and the cedar. Forest soils in which there is a wealth of leaf mold, and that are fairly light in texture, are most favorable to the growth of this plant. It is almost never found in open ground and soon perishes in clearings, but thrives in the half shade afforded by hardwood forests where the undergrowth is scant.

HOW TO BEGIN—STARTING WITH WILD ROOTS.

The easiest way to commence ginseng cultivation is to collect plants in the neighborhood and to transplant them. Dig them either early in the spring just as the new growth begins to appear, or in the autumn, when the tops are dying or have died down. It is hard to collect the plants in the spring, because they look so much like other plants as they are coming through the ground that it is hard to distinguish them, and it is difficult to remove them at this season without injury to the small rootlets that have been produced before the leaves appear. It is better to transplant wild plants in the fall, when the roots are ready for a rest and are not nearly so likely to be injured, besides being much more easily found. It is better to transplant autumn-gathered plants at once than to keep them until spring, although this may be done without trouble or fear of greater loss than when set in the fall. In storing, plunge the roots in damp, not moist or wet, earth in a cool place where they cannot dry out.

An easy way to get a large number of roots in a small space, and without danger of injuring them, is to stand an open box,—a soap box is a handy size,—upon end and tilt it slightly back by putting a brick under the front. Put in a layer of fine earth an inch or so deep at the end, and lay a row of roots upon it so that they do not touch each other. Cover these with earth and put in the next layer of roots; so on until the box is full. Always take care to prevent the roots from touching one another, as contact will hasten the spreading from plant to plant of any decay that may commence. When full, set the box upon its bottom, and fill in any looseness in the packing by adding more soil. When finished, the roots will be in their natural position. Store in a root cellar, separate from the dwelling, if possible, although a house cellar will do if it is not too warm. If the roots become dry they will not grow. If stored in a cool, moist place, such as a root cellar or pit, do not water them, as this might induce rot. **Do not let them freeze**, for though they will stand a low temperature when properly protected in the forest, they are more tender when under unnatural conditions such as would prevail in the box.

If collected in the spring, set the plants in the bed at once; or if they must be kept out of the ground for a few hours, keep them carefully covered with damp soil, to prevent any possible injury to the tender rootlets. The easiest way to dig the plants, when growing in the woods, is to use a small spade, thrusting it straight down at a distance of four or five inches from the plant and to the full depth of the blade. If closer or shallower than this there is danger of breaking the roots, and thus ruining them. A trowel, though useful for transplanting the more evenly developed cultivated roots, is not a good tool to use in the woods, because of the possible presence of other roots, stones and pieces of wood that might interfere with the removal of the root. In the cultivated beds, however, these objections are overcome, and the trowel may be used to advantage in transplanting the seedlings.

Always take the greatest care to preserve the bud at the crown of the root. If destroyed, there will be more or less loss of time, if not of the plants themselves.

STARTING WITH SEED.

When collecting roots, be sure to also collect all seed. Either sow it at once in a previously prepared bed, or store it. Each method has advantages and disadvantages. The only advantage in planting at once is that the seed is permanently disposed of. The disadvantages are that since eighteen months must elapse before the seed can be made to sprout, there is much risk that the seed bed may become dry, and the seed thus be rendered worthless; the seed bed must also be attended to, mulched, shaded, weeded, and protected from chickens, mice and other nuisances. Then there is much more anxiety when the seed is thus handled than when it is stored. If, however, it be stored, the danger of drying can be reduced to a minimum, and the trouble in connection with the bed be all avoided.

If possible, gather the seed while the pulp is still soft, after it is fully ripe and before it becomes dry. Do not, however, throw away any that has become dry in this way, as it may still be of use. Do not remove the pulp, but store it with the seeds intact.

The best way to store the seed is to stratify it. Make a mixture of leaf mold, sand and loam and pass it through a fine sieve, finer than the size of the seed with the pulp off. If not sifted, great difficulty will be experienced in removing the seeds from the mixture when the time comes for planting. A mixture made in this way and sifted will be slower to dry out than most unmixed soils, and will therefore be better as a storage material. Put a layer half an inch deep smoothly upon the bottom of a box and scatter the berries thickly but only one deep upon it. Put in another half inch of earth, then a second layer of berries, and so continue until the box is full. A deep cigar box will hold several ounces of seed and is a handy size to use, although a stronger box will generally be better, particularly where it is to be much exposed to the weather.

When packed, either store the box in a cellar, as described for ginseng roots, or bury it in some place that will not become wet but will always be moist enough to prevent the possibility of drying out in the summer. Since frost does not injure the seeds, but rather improves their germinating qualities, it will be better to put the box out of doors than in the cellar. During the summer it will always be best to bury the seed, to escape the molds that are commonly present in cellars. Care must also be taken to prevent the attacks of mice upon the seeds. A covering of perforated tin or of wire netting will effect this and will not hinder the entrance of rain or other water. The soil and the seeds must not be allowed to become too wet, since the latter may rot.

When the seeds have been stored a year, sift them out, as described below. As some few of the smaller ones may pass through the sieve, the earth in which they have been stored should be scattered over the seed bed in order that they may not be wasted.

An important thing, in the cultivation of this plant, is the annual setting of a seed bed. This must be done regularly, as the plantation grows in extent and age, since neglect to plant only one seed bed will mean the loss of one, perhaps two, or even three crops, because many roots require one or two years longer to attain a marketable size. It will be economy in the end to purchase seed in any one year that furnishes only a small supply or none at all. Under ordinary circumstances, however, this necessity should not occur more than once or twice, and then only in the first few years while the industry is getting upon its feet and before the beds commence to bear seed in any quantity.

CLIMATE AND LOCATION.

From what has been said of the natural home of the plant it may be seen that ginseng will succeed over a wide range of territory. It must not, however, be inferred from this that it can be grown anywhere in this territory. Efforts to grow it in the low lands of the southern states are almost sure to meet with failure, or when failure be prevented it will be at the cost of so much effort that there will be no profit or pleasure in it. The plant demands a cool climate, such as is found in the northern states and in the high lands of both the north and the south. In such places it will grow as easily in cultivated areas as in the forest, provided the proper conditions be furnished.

In choosing locations for beds, particularly in the more southerly states, be sure to give the northern exposure the preference, because the plants will do better where the direct rays of the sun are more or less overcome by the sloping of the land to the north. In such exposures, too, the land is less robbed of moisture. But if the soil and other conditions are unfavorable, or where such an aspect cannot be secured, do not hesitate because an eastern, a western, or even a southern aspect must be utilized. Ginseng will prove profitable, as it has in former cases, provided the necessary care be taken to secure plenty of shade and moisture. Other conditions being equal, however, the northern slope is best and the southern poorest.

SOIL.

Having chosen the location for the bed, the next question, or rather the one that must be considered at the same time as the location question, is the choice of soil. Choose almost any quality or texture, with the exceptions of clay, heavy clay loam, light sand and muck. These are not adapted to the requirements of the plant and its best development. The best soil is a good, friable loam, light rather than heavy, and well supplied with decaying vegetable matter. It must be clear of stones, clods, chunks of wood, tree roots and other obstructions, so that the ginseng roots may have free range to develop and not be robbed of food or be distorted. If the soil be filled with obstructions the roots will often be greatly branched, but if free they will tend to be of more regular shape, and can thus be much more easily dug when the time comes. The difference in shape, in size, and in earliness of maturity between roots grown upon a deep, mellow loam, and those grown upon a heavy soil, is so remarkable that an inexperienced person might easily doubt that each lot sprang from the same seed.

The deeper the soil, the better. It should also be underlaid with some porous subsoil to insure natural drainage, which for this crop, particularly when grown in the woods, is much more desirable than drainage by artificial means. Moreover, artificial drainage of forest beds would often be attended with much inconvenience and expense, owing to the liability of tile or other artificial channels to be clogged by tree roots, especially where elm, willow and such water-loving trees grow not far off.

If the beds be upon the level, as all garden and orchard beds should be, the subsoil should never be clay, hard pan or rock, because, owing to their shallowness, such formations are sure to be too wet in the spring, autumn and winter, and too dry in summer. In the forest these adverse conditions are more or less overcome by the natural mulches of leaves, but even in the woods such situations should be avoided, if possible. In winter, unless the beds be very carefully mulched, the plants will be very liable to be heaved out and destroyed by frost. If, however, the hard subsoil or rock be some inches below the frost line there should be little danger of injury from frost or from drying out in summer, provided the soil be good, and well mulched. If the location of the bed be upon a slope, particularly if it be situated near the top, the presence of an impenetrable subsoil, especially in summer, is of small consequence, since the excess water will be almost sure to drain away naturally before damage could occur.

But while it is important to carry off the excess water, do not suppose that the beds should be dry. Ginseng will not thrive in such soil, while freshly gathered seed planted in it, as already described, and thus exposed during the hot months of summer, will be sure to perish. The most important point to consider, in choosing the soil—even more important than depth, quality and position—is its natural power of holding moisture. Do not understand, by this, that a wet soil is meant; ginseng does not grow naturally in such ground, and will die when stuck in a bog.

To sum up: Choose a moist, mellow, deep loam, rich in decaying vegetable matter, free from obstructions, naturally well drained and preferably facing the north. Such a soil, in such a situation, will be almost sure to be capable of retaining moisture and of giving good return at digging time.

PREPARATION OF THE BEDS.

We are now ready to prepare our plantation. We may dispense with all beds, and trust to nature to do the work. All that is necessary, in this case, is to roughly clear the ground of brush and leaves, scatter and lightly cover the seed, and trust to time. This is the lazy man's method, and is liable to great losses from the drying out of the seed and from the browsing and trampling of animals. It is slow in the extreme. It is therefore condemned, and the following one recommended.

We will need one bed in which to raise seedlings, and another in which to transplant our growing roots. Let us look at the nursery, or seed bed, first. Spare no pains to make it perfect. The best place for it, as in fact for all ginseng beds, is in the forest, where the trees are tall, and where there is no undergrowth to interfere. Fig. 8 presents a photograph of Mr. George Stanton's nursery plantation, where young ginseng plants are raised by the tens of thousands. As will be seen, it is admirably adapted for the purpose to which it is put, the trees being tall, the undergrowth scant, and the shade not too dense.

Fork the ground over thoroughly to the depth of a foot or more, and take out all tree roots and stones that

FIG. 8. FOREST SEED BED WITH ONE HUNDRED THOUSAND SEEDLINGS.

might interfere with the young ginseng plants. It may often occur that the soil, though rich in vegetable matter at the surface, may have practically none lower down than four or five inches. In such cases, give a heavy application of leaf mold and work it in well. Remember that labor thus expended will be well rewarded. Should there be danger of flooding, raise the beds two or three inches, and protect them by boards at the sides and ends. These need be only six inches wide, as a rule, and may be held in place by stakes.

The size of the nursery bed will, of course, be governed by the quantity of seed at hand. Do not make the width more than four feet, because in wide beds the centers are harder to reach than in narrow ones and the difficulty of properly attending to them is thus greater. A bed three or four feet wide will be found best, as every part can be reached with but little exertion. Since the nursery bed is usually small and demands more frequent attention than permanent beds, it will be better to have it narrow than to use the method described later on for attending to the permanent beds. The best situation for a nursery bed in a garden plantation is upon the extreme north of the plot. It will be least exposed to the sun, even when shade is provided.

To calculate the amount of space necessary for a given amount of seed, allow from nine to twelve square feet for each ounce of seed to be sown. The distance between the rows, and the seeds in the rows, mentioned under Planting, will account for the difference in the amount of space required.

In both nursery and permanent beds situated in the forest and in beds set out in orchards or near trees, it will be necessary to cut around the beds each year at least once, to kill any tree roots that may find their way into the ground prepared for ginseng. If neglected only one year, the amount of work to be done the following year

24 THE GINSENG INDUSTRY.

FIG. 9. GARDEN PLANTATION WITH LATTICE SHED.

will be more than double, on account of the larger number, greater strength and size of the roots that will have developed. If attended to regularly each year, the work will be slight and the benefit to the beds much greater.

In locating a bed in an orchard, it is best to avoid proximity to cherry trees, as the plants, for some unexplained reason, do not thrive under this fruit tree. They do well, however, under apple trees. When set under these, it is better to put the bed under late fall or winter apples, because these do not drop to the ground so much during the growing season of ginseng as early apples. Much breakage and consequent injury to the plants may thus be avoided.

PREPARATION OF PERMANENT BEDS.

There need be little difference between the preparation of a permanent bed and that of a nursery bed. The principal differences are in the width of the beds and the texture of the soil. The width of the permanent beds may be as much as six or seven feet, the former width preferred if the beds are situated in the forest, where space is unlimited. But in the garden or in the orchard, where artificial shade must be provided, and where, as a consequence, space must be economized, make them seven or eight feet wide, and the paths between them as narrow as possible. Eighteen inches should be the widest limit. A garden plantation is shown at Fig. 9, to which reference will be made later.

If a wheelbarrow is to be taken into the plantation and the path is not wide enough, the barrow may be run over the beds if the ground be frozen hard enough to bear it up. There will be no necessity to take a wheelbarrow into the plantation at any time during the growing season, because if properly managed there should be no weeds to cart away and no manure to apply. The manuring may all be done in the late fall.

To make weeding in the centers of wide beds easy, place strong boards twelve inches wide on each side of the bed, and when cultivating lay a stout board upon them, to be used as a seat while weeding. Another plan is to use a horse like the one illustrated in Fig. 10, instead of the boards. This should be made high enough to clear the plants.

With regard to the texture of the soil, it has been found that although the seedlings do well in the soil mixture recommended for them, the older plants do not succeed so well when grown continuously in it. The soil for the permanent beds should not be so light that the hand may be plunged into it to the depth of the roots, as in the case of good nursery-bed earth. For permanent beds the soil should be firmer, stronger and deeper. It should resemble good garden loam, but should have more humus than is found in most garden soils.

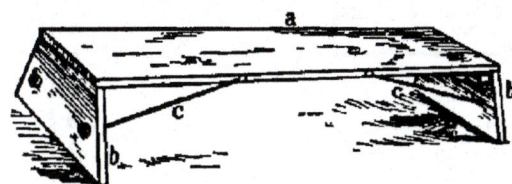

FIG. 10. WEEDING HORSE.
a, Top plank; *b, b*, side pieces, *c, c*, braces.

In such a soil, the time required for the development of good, marketable roots will be less, the texture of the roots will be firmer, and their appearance will be better than when grown in lighter ground. As far as garden beds are concerned, any soil that approaches the quality described above will answer the purpose, provided it will readily retain moisture, and is not too stiff. The bed must be so situated that it can be readily shaded.

PLANTING OF THE SEED.

The statement has been made, that the seed may either be sowed at once or stored. In either case, the following remarks upon planting will hold good. But owing to the greater risk run, and the extra trouble

PLANTING THE SEED.   27

that must be taken to prevent the seeds from drying out in the bed if planted as soon as gathered, it will be much better to store the seeds for one year, as already described.

Set the seeds singly in rows two or three inches apart and at intervals of one or two inches apart in the row. It is important that they receive plenty of moisture, particularly until the little plants appear above the ground. To insure this the seeds should be set about one inch below the surface of the soil. When properly planted, and when sown in the autumn, as recommended, the seeds will require but little attention.

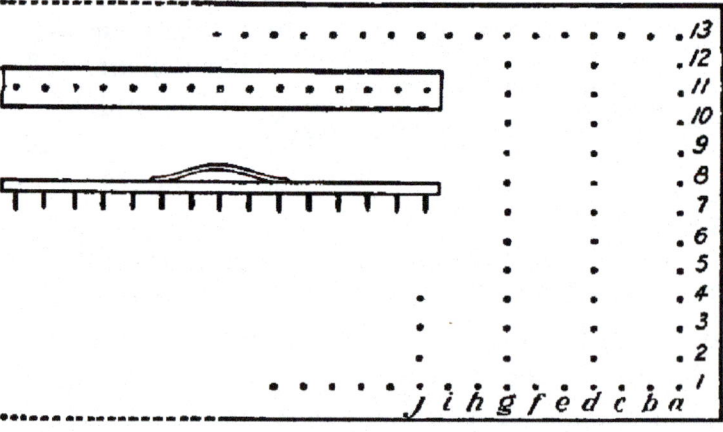

FIG. 11. HANDY MARKER.

Fig. 11 shows a handy tool which will enable the grower to set the seeds very rapidly at the proper depth and the proper interval. Bore three-quarter-inch holes an inch apart in a piece of pine board, say, three-fourths of an inch thick, about three inches wide, and as long as the width of the bed. Fill each hole with a peg long enough to project an inch. When a handle has been added, the tool will be ready to use. Lay it flat across the bed and press down until the pegs have sunk in the ground, making the holes 1, 2, 3, 4, etc., as shown in the sketch. This will give the distances between the plants in the first row across the bed. To get the position of the other rows, place the tool at right angles to the first row, and press it down as before, making the holes *a, b, c,* etc. Skip two of the holes, *b, c,* thus made, and, putting the first peg of the marker in the third hole, *d,* lay the tool parallel to the first row and press it down. And so on to the end of the bed. The seeds may then be dropped in the holes and covered with a little soil. The writer can testify, from long experience with this tool, that double the area can be planted in a given time, that the bed will present a far more even appearance, and that it can be much more easily cultivated than when planted in the ordinary way.

When all the seeds have been planted, cover the entire bed to the depth of an inch with muck or leaf mold, the latter preferred. Then scatter loose brush over it, in order to catch and hold leaves, which will help to protect the seed during the winter. Before growth starts in the spring remove the brush, but let the leaves remain unless a very deep layer has been made. They will act as a summer mulch. The seedlings will in no wise be inconvenienced, but will appear through the leaf covering.

TREATMENT OF SEEDLINGS.

The little plants may be expected to appear about the first of May in the North; probably two, three, or even four weeks earlier in the South. In the cultivated beds they can readily be distinguished from all weeds because of their being in rows, so there need be no mistake when weeding the bed. Commence weeding as soon as there is any weed to be taken out, and continue through the season.

It is not wise to disturb the soil by any cultivation, particularly if the leaf mulch has been left, since this might, and probably would, break the tender little stems and roots. The removal of weeds is the only attention necessary during the growing season, and this, owing to the presence of the leaf mulch, which will prevent weed growth to a large extent, will be only slight labor. When the plants have died down in the autumn, give a dressing of well-rotted horse manure and replace the brush covering. In the second season give the bed the same treatment as during the first, namely, remove the brush in the spring and the weeds during the summer.

In the second autumn transplant the young plants to the permanent beds, after the digging of the roots has been completed in October. Trimming should be done only when the roots are much injured in the digging and seem unlikely to recover. After replanting, they must be covered with muck or leaf mold in the same manner as they were the previous seasons in the nursery beds.

The advantages of setting the plants in the autumn are that they have already prepared for winter, and what little injury they may suffer in the digging and transplanting will be callused over long before spring opens. Moreover, the work may be done at any leisure time the grower may have between the dying down of the tops and the advent of frost. If left until the spring, however, the rush of other work may prevent the transplanting until the plants have grown so much that injury may result. But there is no other objection to setting in the spring if this be preferred, and the grower need not wait until the plants have appeared above ground, because if the bed has been properly laid out he can lay his hand upon them at any time, and may set them as early as the ground will permit, the earlier the better.

It is generally only a matter of convenience, when the cultivated beds are employed, whether the planting be done in the spring or in the fall. And this is a distinct advantage they possess over beds set with wild roots, which generally suffer considerably from injuries to their fibrous roots, with which they are usually rather poorly supplied.

TREATMENT OF PERMANENT BEDS.

The treatment of the permanent bed differs little from that of the nursery bed. The roots must, however, be set farther apart. It has been found that, for roots from two to four years old, a distance of about five inches apart each way is sufficient. For older roots increase the distance. A common garden trowel is the best tool for setting the plants, and the tool illustrated in Fig. 11, but with the pegs made longer and set farther apart, will be found useful in marking the position of the plants in the beds. After setting the roots the beds must be kept clear of weeds, mulched with leaf mold or muck, like the nursery beds, and covered with brush each autumn, as before. It will usually take from three to five years from the transplanting of the two-year-old seedlings to obtain marketable roots. With certain specimens and under certain cultural conditions this time will be greater and the profit will consequently be less. This question will, however, be more fully discussed under the heading, Selection for Improvement.

ARTIFICIAL PROPAGATION.

It has already been shown that ginseng propagates itself only by means of its seeds. But a method of artificial propagation may often be practiced with the older roots. After three years of growth in the cultivated beds they frequently develop side roots near the crown, as already shown in Fig. 7, which, if carefully removed with a sharp knife and planted immediately, may be made to grow. When they succeed, which they will do if properly handled, they may produce seed the first season after being divided, and the roots will grow to a marketable size much sooner than seedlings. Often two, or even more, years may be gained by this method with individual roots. By this is meant only that after the roots have been separated and grown in the bed two or three seasons they may be large enough to dig for drying.

PROTECTION OF THE BEDS.

The first protection, in a ginseng plantation, is the protection against thieves. The root commands so high a price and is so energetically sought, that if the beds be situated where ginseng hunters can have access to them the profits of growing the crop will be small indeed. In Kentucky, where the root is very largely gathered in the woods, numerous cases are upon record of men growing several thousand roots to a marketable size, only to have them stolen a few days before they intended digging them themselves. Usually they have not attempted to grow them again, but sometimes they concluded, from the appearance of the plants and their method of handling them, that they could make money by guarding them, and have built fences and shelters around their beds, and have even employed watchmen profitably. The average "sang" digger has very little conscience, and questions not whether the roots are cultivated and rightfully belong to another. Therefore, unless the grower can place his beds beyond the sight and reach of the professional hunter of this root, he had better not attempt ginseng cultivation.

Protection against cattle and sheep is next in importance. All grazing stock, and probably deer, are fond of the leaves of this plant and the beds must be protected against them if they are allowed free range in the woods where the beds are located. Even animals not partial to the leaves may do considerable injury by trampling over the beds if left unprotected. The best kind of fence is a matter that the grower must decide for himself.

The third protection is the mulch. Keep it upon the bed both summer and winter. In the hot months let it be light and shallow, but deep enough to check the evaporation of moisture from the soil. In the cold months make the mulch deep, so as to prevent all possibility of the roots being injured by frost. For these purposes there is nothing better than leaves, which are the natural coverings of the plants at both seasons. And there is no better way of collecting and holding them in place than by the brush covering already spoken of.

MANURING.

If the soil be naturally fertile, little or no manuring will be necessary for the first crop. But for later crops, and upon soils not already well supplied with plant food, a dressing of well-rotted horse manure may be used advantageously. Avoid fresh manure as much as possible; but where no rotted manure can be obtained and only fresh can be had, spread it in the autumn after the tops of the plants have died down, and only then. It should then do no harm, but if applied fresh in the spring, there is danger of the plants becoming injured by contact with strong solutions of the manure, particularly while the plants are very young and are just pushing through the soil.

Potash salts and phosphates have been experimented with to a limited extent, and have been found beneficial. But for general plantations, well-rotted horse manure at the rate of about one wheelbarrow load to fifty square feet upon ordinary soil will be found sufficient. If potash is to be given, choose the sulphate in preference to the muriate, as the latter sometimes has an injurious effect upon certain soils and the former does not. Phosphoric acid may be applied in the form of ground bone or the superphosphate. Unleached wood ashes from hardwood trees may be applied in the autumn and will often benefit the plants. Such manures should, however, be used with great caution, as they are very strong, and if applied too liberally are likely to injure the plants, particularly while young.

If the soil be very rich, dense, and retentive of fertility, make the applications of stable manure lighter than mentioned, or withhold them altogether; if poor, sandy and leachy, let them be heavier, even double the amount specified. But try to avoid soils that demand large quantities of fertilizer, because they will usually be unsuited to this crop in other ways.

SHADES AND SHADING.

The natural shade of the forest is always better than any artificial shade that can be produced. This must not, however, be too dense. The best way to secure the proper degree of shade in the forest plantation is to remove all the smaller growth for a space of twenty feet from the margins of the beds. This, besides reducing the drain made upon the soil by the roots of these saplings, will leave the taller trees to supply the shade, and if they are not too bare of limbs they will give sufficient.

But where forest beds cannot be laid out, be sure to provide an artificial shade of some kind. This may be supplied in several ways. Perhaps the simplest that suggests itself to the beginner is the growing of some hardy perennial climbers upon frames above the plants. But this generally requires too much time to produce a sufficient shade, and too much plant food is likely to be taken from the soil by the climbers. It is therefore not recommended.

A second plan is the growing of annual climbers upon strings. For this method make the beds run east and west, and plant such seeds as Yosemite wax, scarlet runner or other climbing beans, morning glories and Japanese variegated hop along the south margin. Set light, ten-foot posts on the north side of the beds, deep enough in the ground to secure support to the light poles nailed across their tops and to the vines to be grown. At the surface of the ground fasten a strip of narrow board firmly with stakes parallel to the bed. Before setting the board in place, drive stout tacks almost full length into the board, to which fasten the strings. By using a little ingenuity, much labor may be saved in putting up the strings. One way is to tie the string at the first tack at the bottom end of the bed, and having the twine in a ball, stretch it to the first tack at the top, giving it a wind around this tack, and carrying it to the next one, again winding it and carrying to the second tack below. Repeat the process until the whole is done, and fasten the string to the last tack.

The climbers mentioned are all rapid growers, and when sown early, in rich soil, should produce a good shade long before the hot weather sets in. This plan allows of perfect freedom in the management of the bed, but is open to the objection that it is not permanent and necessitates reconstruction each year, and unless sheltered from strong winds is likely to suffer. There is also some slight loss of fertility, due to the feeding of the plants upon the ginseng beds, and often much trouble from the seedlings that may spring up in the bed and become weeds. This last is the main objection to the plan. But in the case of the beans it might be made of small account, as the pods could be removed before they dropped their seed. If an edible bean be planted, a crop could be secured from the plants.

Probably the best artificial shade is made with laths. These, for economy and ease in handling, should be made in square sections, as shown in Fig. 12. Lay two laths parallel to each other and the length of a lath apart. Lay other laths upon and between them at intervals of an inch and fasten them to the first pair with clinch nails. The section may be made extra strong by interweaving a lath across the slats, as shown in the sketch. In the spring, before the plants begin to appear, tie these sections to a framework of scantling

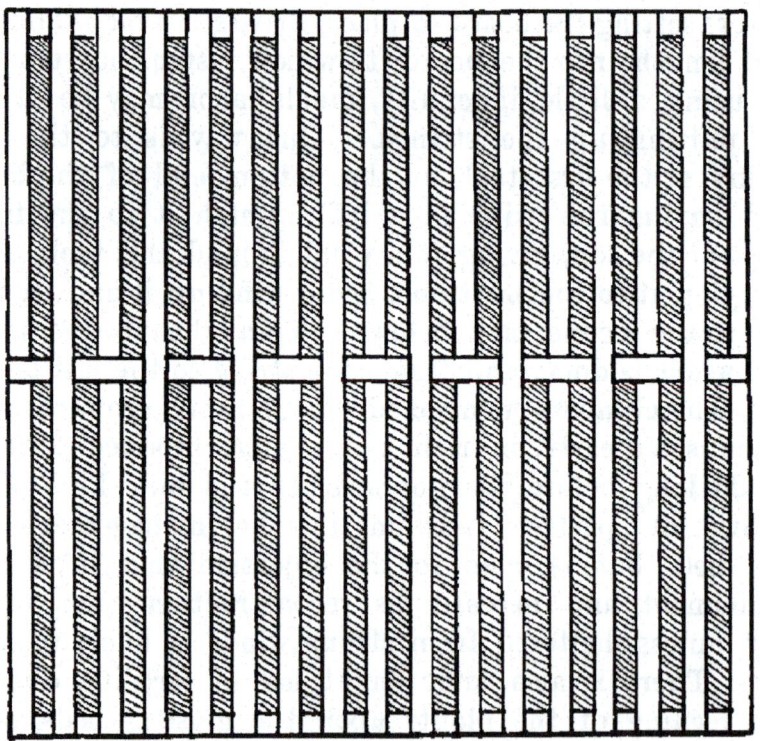

FIG. 12. LATH SCREEN FOR SHADE.

raised upon posts high enough from the ground to permit of standing erect under it. See Fig. 9 for completed shade.

In October remove and store the sections in some dry place. They may thus be made to last longer than when exposed. Since, in regions where the snowfall is heavy, many sections would likely be broken if left in place during the winter, they should not be left exposed to the weather and to decay. Again, when they are removed there is better chance for leaves to collect upon the beds and to protect them. Along the sides of the bed exposed to the direct rays of the sun it will be found necessary to place a vertical shade, to protect those parts of the bed from the summer sun.

A modification of this plan is to make the framework for the sections just high enough from the ground to clear the plants by a few inches. With the smaller plants, about fifteen inches, and with the larger about thirty inches, will usually be about right. In this method the sections are not fastened to the frame, but only held in place by stones or other weights, which can easily be removed when the bed is to be weeded or otherwise attended. The plan is not so good as the preceding one, since there is likely to be too much shade in some spots and not enough in others, and there will always be more or less annoyance and loss of time in having to lift the sections out of the way when attending to the plants.

ENEMIES.

So far as can be learned, ginseng has no specific enemy. A few insects and snails may occasionally be found upon its leaves, and sometimes trouble has been caused by worms at the roots, but this latter has been only when the roots have been attacked by some kind of decay, the products of which, and not the roots themselves, were attractive to the creatures. With the exception of this decay there seem to be no diseases that attack the plant, a point well worth noting. It is probable, too, that the decay is caused by injury of some kind to the roots, since it has not been noticed in cultivated beds except very rarely.

Injury is often done by moles and mice. The moles do not attack the plants, but merely make tunnels through the beds and thus disturb the plants. It is likely that the moles do as much good as harm, since they eat a great many worms and grubs that might injure the plants. If the grubs were not present the moles would not give any trouble, because they would seek places better supplied with food. Mice are charged with eating the roots, whether justly or not it is hard to say. But since they give trouble by making nests and burrows in the beds, they are nuisances and should be kept in check. The usual methods of catching both moles and mice will apply to the ginseng bed pests. Dogs, cats, poison and traps are all useful.

Chickens should be kept away from the beds, because they are sure to be grateful to the grower for preparing so nice a place to scratch. They are also said to be fond of the berries when these are ripe. There are cheaper chicken foods than ginseng berries at a dollar an ounce for the seed.

SELECTION FOR IMPROVEMENT.

A point that should be considered by every grower of this root, is the improvement of his stock. This, it seems probable, can be accomplished by the practice of methods successfully applied in the improvement of other cultivated plants. Care and patience are the two principal requisites.

Select the best specimens and grow them in a bed by themselves, giving them a little extra attention. Save the plants and the seed they mature separate from the general crop, and when the plants so produced are large enough to judge of their qualities, select those that seem the best, and transplant the poorer ones to the general market bed. Save and plant the seed from the superior ones, as before, and so continue.

By choosing the best formed, the earliest maturing and the largest roots, these qualities may be imparted to

FIG. 13. IRREGULAR ROOTS.

the descendants, and by selecting seed from plants that produce it soonest or in largest amount, these qualities may be perpetuated. By combining these points, selecting the all-round best variety, propagating from it and discarding all those that do not approach the ideal, such as shown in Fig. 13, the proportion of superior specimens to inferior will gradually increase until the valuable characteristics become fixed and a variety becomes established.

It is confidently believed that as great changes can be wrought in the character of the ginseng plant as have been brought about, for instance, in the carrot, which in its wild state is a noxious weed. This change would include, among other things, a reduction in time between seeding and harvest, an increased proportion of large to small roots obtained from any given quantity of seed, and an improvement in the form, size and weight of the specimens themselves. Further, a variety known to possess valuable characters will always command a higher price among planters, and the originator of such a variety could thus be paid for his time and trouble. In a plant of such slow growth as ginseng, a variety that would take one-half the time to produce a marketable root should be worth at least double the price of ordinary seed or young plants for setting, and the same should be true of the qualities of size, form, weight and increased seed production, the superior variety always commanding the higher price.

It may be noted that large seed will usually germinate in advance of small, produce more thrifty plants, larger roots, and perhaps show flowers and seeds before plants raised from smaller seed subjected to the same conditions. This should also be looked after in the selection of superior kinds.

If, on the other hand, the method of selection recommended for market roots be practiced (as it generally is where any method is practiced at all), instead of the method described above, the result will be a reduction in the amount and the quality of the seed, a diminution in the size and the quality of the roots produced, and an increase in the time required to grow them to a marketable size. The same results will be apparent when no method at all is followed, though in a somewhat less degree. These results will become more evident as the years advance, the roots getting smaller and taking longer each generation.

CULTIVATED VERSUS WILD ROOT.

For export, select the largest and heaviest roots and make them perfectly clean. Such ginseng is in greatest demand and commands the highest price. Unless specimens in some remote degree resemble the human form, the less they are branched the better. If roots be found that in any way look like the human body, wash and cure them with extra care and keep them separate from the rest, as the Chinese value them far more highly than the ordinary roots. In general, however, look to size, form, weight and smoothness. These are most frequently found in the cultivated roots, and are due largely to transplanting. This practice tends to produce many fibrous roots, instead of a few large branching ones. The main advantage of this is that the rootlets readily snap off in the drying, thus leaving a smooth shaft but little defaced by their removal.

Cultivated roots require less time in drying and suffer less shrinkage in the process than wild roots, and on account of their better appearance,—being whiter and clearer (translucent),—they command a higher price in the market than the wild. In 1897 a New York grower sold his crop for $1.50 more than the market quotation ($4.50), for the best quality of wild root from his state. This figure was then unusual, in fact the highest paid for many years. Six dollars have been offered several times last season for cultivated root. And it may be taken as a general rule that dealers, in buying ginseng, or in fact any commodity, will give a higher price for the better grades of roots, whether cultivated or wild. The former certainly is much superior to the latter, as generally offered.

Again, it is believed that the distinction made with regard to the locality in which the root grows would frequently be set aside, and a higher price paid for the produce of the beds than for wild root from the same locality, or even a more favored region. For instance, southern root is quoted low, and northern high, because the former is poorer both in size and in appearance. But if ginseng were cultivated in the south it might be expected to command not only higher prices than are usually offered for wild roots from its locality, but prices equal to or greater than those offered for northern wild root.

PREPARATION FOR MARKET.

In digging, which is the first step in the preparation of the root for market, be careful to take up the roots without breaking them, since whole roots command higher prices than mutilated ones. If the digging be started at one end of the bed, taking only one row at a time, by putting the spade on the outside, less injury should occur than if the plants were dug from the end of the row or from the inside of it. Digging may be commenced as soon as the plants have died down in the autumn, only large roots being selected for drying. Replant all the undersized ones in a bed previously prepared for them. By undersized is meant all roots weighing less than, say, two ounces. This method will save work in washing and drying, the roots will suffer less shrinkage in drying, will command a higher price because of their better size and uniformity, and for the same reason will become recognized by the dealer who handles them as of superior quality, thus gaining his confidence.

Large quantities of good root are annually injured in value by careless handling after they are taken from the beds; therefore, pay particular attention to the following: Shake off all loose earth and place the roots at once in water, so that the earth remaining upon them may not become dry, and thus stick to the roots. When all are dug, put them in a tub with plenty of water, and wash them thoroughly in several waters, using a rather stiff broom, but be careful not to break the roots. Use a hand brush to finish any specimens that are not perfectly clean after the washing in the tub. The roots are now ready to be dried.

Drying in the sun is too slow a process, and though practiced to a large extent by the sang diggers, it is useful only for summer-dug roots, the sun not being warm enough when the roots are dug at the proper season. The practice of drying the roots in an oven, or in pans upon the top of the stove, is usually too rapid, and there is much danger of burning them when dried in this way. The value of many roots is reduced by drying them on strings hung in the kitchen. In this way they become more or less discolored, and are considered inferior on account of the holes made in them by the strings. As the roots run such great risks of being cooked when dried in the oven or upon the stove, it will be found best to rely upon a more gentle heat. Nothing is better than to dry them in a current of warm air. This may be secured in either of the two simple homemade dryers described herewith.

Get a box large enough to cover the top of the kitchen stove, and deep enough to hold six or eight sliding shelves. Remove the bottom entirely. Make a hole in the top; take off one side, and make a hinged door to fit in its place; make a number of shelves with bottoms of wire netting of about one-fourth inch mesh. In filling the trays for the first time, put the largest roots in the top trays and the smallest upon the bottom ones, the lowest of which should be at least six inches above the top of the stove. Place the box upon the stove, but raised about half an inch above it, so as to prevent its bottom edges from becoming scorched, and to insure a current of air through the shelves of roots. A few stout nails left projecting above the edges will accomplish this end. Fill the trays and place them in the dryer; do not have a roaring fire. The heat given off from an ordinary cook stove after the dinner has been removed will be about right for this kind of dryer. Remember, it is warm, and not hot, air that gives best results in drying. The objections to this dryer are that it is often in the way of the housewife, and that it must frequently be removed to accommodate her, thus losing much time in the necessarily slow process of curing the roots. If a separate stove can be used for it, it will be found a first-class apparatus.

If wood be used for fuel and the stove pipe passes through an upper room that may be used for the purpose, a good dryer may be made to fit around the pipe. Or where the house is heated by a furnace, a portable dryer may be made to fit over a register. Failing these, the grower may readily construct a serviceable dryer to work upon the principle of a warm air current through the roots, that will meet his individual needs. A shelf containing two hundred square inches of netting should hold about two pounds of green roots, and should last for at least five years if properly cared for. The whole dryer should not cost more than ten dollars for time and materials necessary to build it.

No rule as to the time required in drying can be given, since roots of the same size differ greatly as to their time of curing; solid and cultivated roots require less time than wild and spongy ones. The degree of heat maintained in the dryer, and the volume of air that passes through it in a given time, also influence the time required. Never try to shorten this time by splitting or cutting the roots. This lowers their market value.

The roots upon the lowest shelf will ordinarily dry first. Take them out, fill the tray with fresh roots and put it in the dryer at the top, after moving all the other trays down one notch toward the bottom. In this way the greatest good may be obtained from the same quantity of heat, and the time of drying may be considerably reduced. In drying, the cultivated roots suffer somewhat less from shrinkage than the wild ones, which lose about two-thirds of their weight. The former are, therefore, more profitable to dry.

The fibrous matter, which is usually more abundant upon the cultivated than upon the wild root, will of course become brittle long before the root itself becomes dry. This is of no value for export, and, if left on, as it generally is by the southern diggers, reduces the price paid for the article. It must therefore be trimmed off, by rubbing the roots gently between the hands. When smooth, return the trimmed roots to the dryer to become completely dry. Save the trimmings, however, since they may often be sold at the drug stores for enough to pay the cost of trimming, or even more. They are used to supply the people who like to chew ginseng. A dried and trimmed root is shown in Fig. 14.

When the large roots have become as dry as a bone and are perfectly cool, put them in paper sacks or clean boxes to await shipment. This should take place as early as possible, provided a good price may be obtained, because if kept for any great length of time there is danger of their becoming infested with boring beetles.

PREPARATION FOR MARKET. 45

These little creatures would soon ruin the roots completely if allowed entrance. If the roots, owing to low

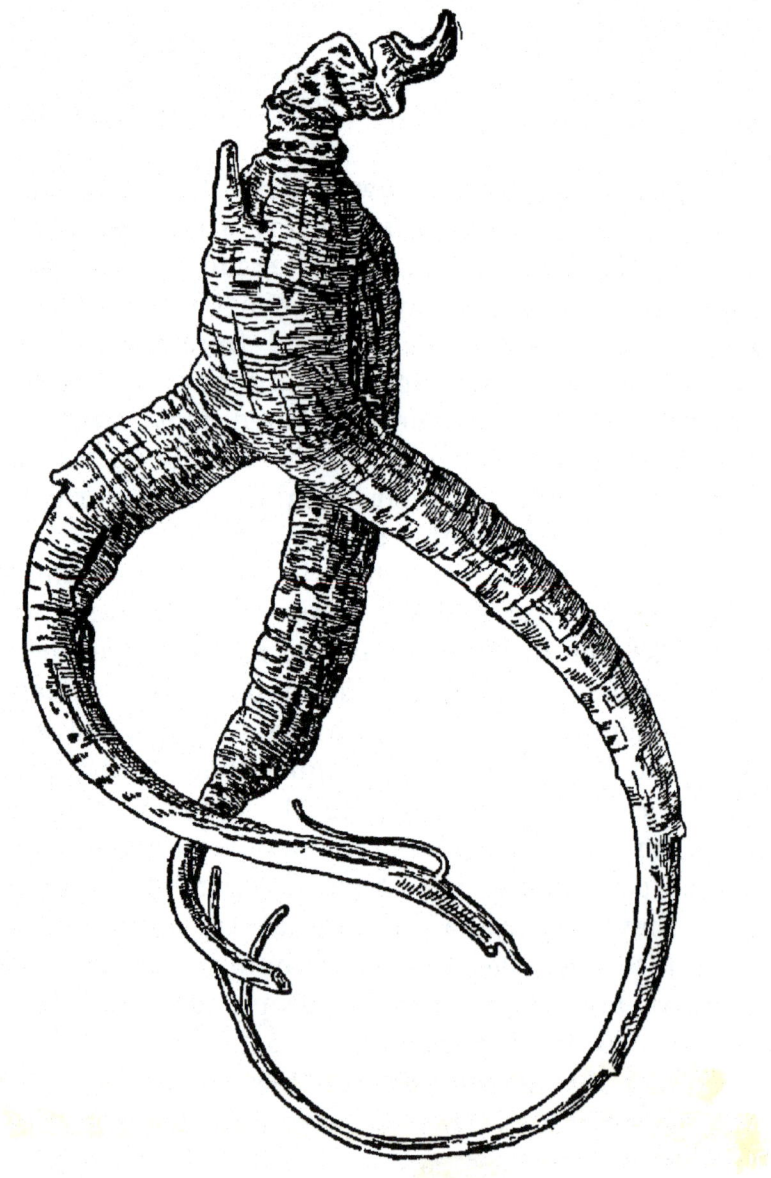

FIG 14 DRIED ROOT.

market prices, must be kept from one season to the next, they should be put in tight tins or glass jars, so as to prevent the entrance of the beetles. The quality of the roots is not injured by being kept over from one season to the next. Not even an expert would know the difference between the freshly dried root and that dried a year or two earlier.

Should insects, by any accident, obtain entrance, put the roots in a tight can and place a small cup in the top. Pour some carbon bisulphide into the cup, about a tablespoonful for a two-gallon can. Close the vessel up tight for, say, a week. Carbon bisulphide is a liquid that quickly becomes a gas of very poisonous properties. It must never be handled at night, and no light of any kind must be allowed near it, because it is as inflammable as gunpowder. If ginseng be properly taken care of, however, there will be but little need of this poison being used upon it.

In shipping, be sure to separate the roots into grades, depending upon size, smoothness and weight, the largest being by themselves, and the smallest by themselves, in clean packages. This grading will often pay for the actual work two or three times over, whereas, if it be not done the roots will sell at about the price that the smallest grade should bring. Mark every package in a conspicuous place with the grade, the quantity, and your name and address. Pack the bags or small boxes tightly in large, strong boxes, so as to avoid any breakage of the roots while being handled on their way to market. Address the box to the best dealer in ginseng that you know.

Above all things, have everything clean, roots, bags and boxes. It will pay well.

PROFITS.

The reader is by this time more than curious to know what money may be made in the growing of this crop, and first asks as to the demand. According to official commerce reports published by the Bureau of

Statistics of the United States Treasury Department, we exported during the fiscal year ending June 30,

YEAR.	Pounds.	Valued at	Average per lb
1858	366,055	$193,796	$0.52
1868	370,066	380,454	1.02
1878	421,395	497,247	1.17
1888	308,365	657,358	2.13
1889	271,228	634,091	2 33
1890	223,113	605,233	2 71
1891	283,000	959,998	3.39
1892	228,916	803,529	3.51
1893	251,205	792,928	3.15
1894	194,564	619,114	3 18
1895	233,236	826,713	3 54
1896	199,436	770,673	3.86
1897	179,573	846,686	4 71
1898	174,063	836,446	3.66

These figures show the great advance made in prices during the last forty years. Though the quantity has declined, the price has constantly advanced. This increase is best shown by the exports of the last eleven years. In 1898 the quantity exported is approximately only three-fifths of that shipped in 1888, but the average price per pound has advanced to approximately seven times the price offered in 1858, and nearly one and three-quarter times that of eleven years ago.

A glance at the prices paid by the dealers will perhaps be of greater interest. Messrs. Samuel Wells & Co., of Cincinnati, Ohio, furnished figures to the Department of Agriculture for the years 1889 to 1896 inclusive, to which are added those of the years 1897 and 1898 through their courtesy.

YEAR.	Fair.	Choice.
1889	$2.40	$3 40
1890	2.75	4.00
1891	2 50	3.50
1892	2 50	3 50
1893	2.25	3 50
1894	2.42	3.65
1895	2 68	3 75
1896	2.97	3 96
1897	2.60	3 80
1898	2 77	4.64

These figures give a general idea of the run of prices paid by the dealers, but do not show what is paid in the different sections of the country. These, as will be seen from the following table, vary greatly. The difference in prices is due to the actual quality of the root, which in the north is generally solid and well cleaned, but which in the south is often spongy and improperly prepared for market, both in the washing away of earth and in the removal of fine roots. These all help to lower the price.

It may here be remarked that though the prices paid for ginseng have been upon the increase, the profits of the collector have, in reality, been growing less, on account of the greater difficulty in obtaining wild roots of marketable size. It is, however, a hopeful sign for the grower.

The table, which has been compiled from the prices offered in October, 1898, by northern dealers in this root, gives the highest and lowest figures paid for roots from the regions mentioned. These prices are based upon the quality of the root, and it is no uncommon thing for higher prices than are mentioned in this table to be paid for exceptionally fine samples such as ginseng cultivators have to offer.

New York, Vermont, Delaware and Canadian,	$5 00	$5 50
Michigan and Northern Pennsylvania,	4 50	5 25
Wisconsin, Iowa and Minnesota,	3.50	4.50
Ohio, Indiana and Illinois,	3.50	4 00
West Virginia and Southern Pennsylvania,	3 00	4.50
Kentucky and Tennessee,	2.75	3.10

The prices offered in southern markets could not be obtained, as no southern dealers are known to the writer. It is probable, however, that they offer somewhat higher prices than northern dealers can afford to give for southern root. As a rule, the price paid for the southern article in the northern markets is lower than for northern-grown ginseng.

The above table mentions nothing of the prices paid

for the cultivated root, the supply as yet being too small to quote separately. It may, therefore, be interesting to examine the results attained by Mr. George Stanton, the pioneer grower of this root in America. He furnished the following details to *American Agriculturist*:

"The season of 1898 was fairly favorable for ginseng culture, though the early part of the season was rather wet, which resulted in some loss of plants and roots from rot, while drouth in June and July was unfavorable to best development of seed crop. But taken altogether, I have no reason to complain. Plants in garden were splendid, many thousand standing 20 to 30 inches high, spreading 20 to 28 inches from tip to tip of leaves, with magnificent seed heads, presenting a very showy appearance when ripening; plants with 20 and 25 leaflets predominating, and a considerable number of roots producing twin plants. One root taken up in the fall of '97 weighed five ounces, and had germs [buds] for five separate and distinct plants. I put it back into the ground, and the past season it sent up five nice plants with five perfect seed heads. Shall let it grow three or four seasons and note results. Four plants to one root is the most I had ever observed before.

"Ginseng responds to good treatment. The seed crop from less than 24 rods of ground was about 30 pounds, or about 240,000 seeds. I have, at present time, about 30 square rods of ground stocked with root in garden under artificial shade, about 75,000 seedling roots in forest nursery, and about 120,000 seeds to be sown next fall to produce plants in spring of 1900.

"My grounds, up to present time, have produced 165 pounds of dry, marketable root, which sold for $900, the product of less than 10 square rods of ground in 11 years. Not a large showing for the time, I admit. I could have done much better on this line but for the demands for stock for cultivation. The crop of 1898, from two and one-half square rods ground, was 38 pounds dry root; 34 pounds sold for $7 per pound.

"Ginseng culture has come to stay. Many plantations are starting up in many parts of the United States. I made a visit to the eastern part of New York state recently, where I found quite a number of cultivators. Some of them had been engaged in the business ten years. I paid one party $66 for seed, and $152 for his crop of ginseng the past season. Also paid a lady in Wisconsin $38 for seed, and $11 to another in New York state for cultivated ginseng. I give these facts to show that others can make, and are making, a success of ginseng culture."

Of course this is a somewhat remarkable showing. It owes much of its success to the untiring efforts and wide experience of Mr. Stanton. Still, by following carefully the instructions given in this book the beginner should, barring accident, be able to make a good profit. It is, however, well to be cautious and patient, and to be content to extend the plantation as experience dictates, rather than to rush into the business upon a large scale without sufficient knowledge of the details essential to its success. It is, consequently, unsafe to take the figures given above, and to calculate from them the probable returns per acre.

There is great promise in the industry. Though Chinese ginseng is considered by the Chinese as superior to the American variety, there is, nevertheless, a steady sale for the latter. The demand is large; the natural supply is inadequate, and decreasing; the cultivated beds are not being extended fast enough to supply the deficiency in the wild root; the price is consequently high and likely to rise still higher, and, should a glut occur, a very unlikely contingency under the conditions that have prevailed for some years, or should lower prices rule for a time, there need be no cause for alarm.

Leave the plants right in the beds and they will continue to improve in both size and quality, and will be worth more when they are offered for sale.

These considerations have much in them that should appeal to the would-be ginseng grower,—more forcibly than many other crops could. It is, therefore, safe to conclude that with proper attention to the few necessary details—for they are in reality few in number when compared with those of many other crops—good profits may be made in the growing and the marketing of American ginseng.

PART TWO.

PRESENT STATUS OF THE GINSENG INDUSTRY.

PRESENT STATUS OF THE INDUSTRY.

BOTANY OF THE PLANT.

Since the writing of Part I, the most important peculiarity that has been discovered in the ginseng plant is the occasional development of sterile blossoms. Professor Garman, Botanist of the Agricultural Experiment Station of Kentucky, states the case clearly in the following letter published by Mr. J W. Sears in a recent circular: "The ginseng you have sent me appears to be the same species as that grown by you. Only one botanical species is recognized in this country, unless we include the small species with globular root, mentioned in my bulletin. The truth appears to be that *Panax quinquefolium* sometimes produces separate staminate and pistillate flowers and if one happens to get the staminate only he will of course get no fruit. Your plants appear to bear perfect flowers, that is, with both stamens and pistils in the same flower, and hence they produce berries whether other plants are near them or not."

Under what conditions staminate or male plants appear in a plantation is not yet determined, but that they do appear and are not uncommon is a fact that should lead to careful observation on the part of growers. If the discovery be made as to peculiarities of soil, fertilizers, management or other conditions that produce them, the grower may have the control in his own hands so that he may or may not obtain seed as he desires. With seed at present prices the discovery of the causes that influence the production of male plants should alone be sufficient spur to make growers take careful observations. But the discovery may be of still greater value after the decline of the exorbitant prices for seed and plantlets—when the business settles from its present nursery basis to a basis founded upon the market value of the dried root.

To judge from the behavior of asparagus and some other plants in which the staminate individuals are more productive than the pistillate, or at least are so claimed to be by growers, there is reason to believe that the staminate ginseng plants might produce larger roots than pistillate plants. It seems logical to conclude that the plant that bears a full crop of berries should not at the same time produce a large root and

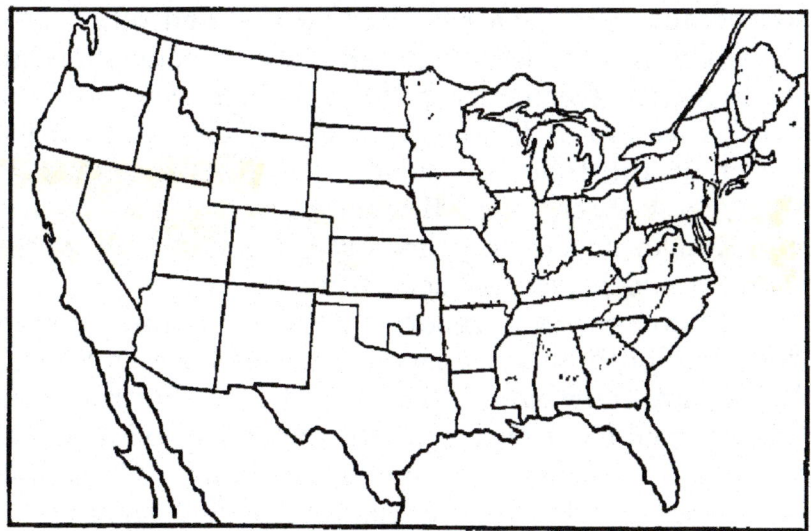

FIG 15. MAP SHOWING THE NATURAL RANGE OF THE GINSENG PLANT IN THE UNITED STATES

also that the plant that does not produce berries should direct its extra energies to increasing the size of its root. At any rate, the matter is one well worth the while of every grower to determine for himself.

BOTANY OF THE PLANT.   57

In this connection also it may be well to call attention here to Mr. Stanton's statements with respect to pinching off the blossoms. There is not the slightest doubt that Mr. Stanton is correct. But, the pinching must be done, as Mr. Stanton says, while the flower-head is scarcely more than a bud.

The natural range of ginseng in the United States is shown in the accompanying map (Fig. 15), prepared by the author for the Division of Botany, United States Department of Agriculture. The shaded portion shows the natural range of ginseng.

Mr. Sears says in one of his circulars that "on some seed-heads one or two rows of berries at the bottom of the head will get ripe first, and with a little care they may be gathered without knocking off any that are green." Other growers think this is a risky operation because green berries may be knocked off.

Some readers have had difficulty in understanding the sentence commencing "The whole work of the plant" (see top of Page 8). The matter may be made clearer by the following sentence: During each year of the first three years the energies of the plant are employed in developing the solitary bud that produces the stem and leaves of each ensuing year

"Many growers report that their roots, coming from the South, will not ripen their seed in this State." We do not know where the absurd idea that southern ginseng could not thrive in the North, or vice versa, ever got a foothold in an intelligent mind. Of course the changing of climatic conditions will disarrange the growth of the plant temporarily, but just as soon as the plant gets accustomed to its new surroundings it will partake of the characteristics of that section, and it is all false to claim that it will not thrive. If it does not thrive it means inattention or ignorance on the part of the cultivator.

In comment on the above quotations and also

upon a similar item which appears in a communication from Mr. Payson it may be well to call attention to the fact that southern grown plants of the same species and even of the same variety are slower in reaching maturity than when grown in the North, because the southern season is longer than the northern. Two instances will illustrate these points: Southern corn brought to Michigan direct from the Gulf States could not be made to ripen its seed; but when planted for a series of years at places removed each year or so farther and farther from the South, seed was obtained at last from plants grown in Michigan. The reverse is true of Michigan corn taken to the South; it grows rapidly and ripens its seed far in advance of the southern varieties planted at the same time, but in a few years it loses its earliness and becomes like other southern varieties.

With ginseng it is the same; the character of the plant will appear in the seedlings and will disappear only after these or their descendants have been grown for a series of years under the changed surroundings. The change is merely an adaptation to climatic conditions. It would be well, therefore, to buy seeds and plants, not merely that have been grown in the North, but that have been grown in the North *from northern seed*. It seems probable that the New York plants referred to by Mr. Payson were grown from southern seed planted in New York State. The difference of three weeks between the time of ripening of their seed and the seed of Canadian plants treated like them, seems too great to be accounted for in any other way, New York and Southern Ontario being approximately alike in climate.

HOW TO BEGIN

It will be noticed in reading the letters from growers in connection with what is said on Page 14, that practice favors autumn planting. Mr. Payson modifies the method of stratifying seed mentioned on Page 17, by having his boxes shallow for the reason that some of the seeds germinate in the spring following their harvest. This seems good practice. As to stratifying berries or only the seed, growers disagree. There seems no reason to suppose that either method is likely to result unfavorably.

A word to all seems necessary as to the so-called "water test" for the goodness of seed. The assumption is that when seed is dropped in water the good will sink and the bad will float. It does not follow, however, that the heavy is necessarily good nor that the light is necessarily bad. A careful test of many kinds of seeds adapted to this method will show that many of the seeds that float will remain at the surface because a tiny bubble holds them there. And many more will float because they are dry. Those that sink may do so because they are specifically heavier than water. This matter is brought up not to cast any discredit upon the water test nor upon the men that advertise that they use it, but to emphasize the fact that among the floating seeds will probably be found many that will produce plants, as also among the heavy ones seeds that will not. If the dealer wish to be scrupulously honest let him sell the heavier seeds and plant the light ones—just for fun. No one can deny him this little pleasure.

SOIL

In reference to the natural home of the plant and to the soil (discussed on Pages 14 and 19) a good piece of evidence is furnished by the Reverend W. H. Kerr, of Crawfordsville, Indiana. He also describes a handy tool for the digging of wild ginseng. The quotation is from *Special Crops* and serves to emphasize what will be said under "Adulteration and Fraud" contradicting the statements of certain persons concerning the places where ginseng will grow. Mr. Fraser also mentions something of the same kind in his letter on a succeeding page.

"There were professional 'sang diggers,' who for the purpose [of digging] used a small hoe, about one and one-half inches wide, by five in length, with a handle two feet long. The hoe was made narrow, to enable the operator to extract the root whole from between the roots of the trees where it was so often found. I never saw it growing on the mountain tops, nor in the swamps, nor in the open, or among the weeds, but in well-drained, rich, loose soil, beneath dense foliage. The green root was prepared for market by being strung on threads and hung by the old-fashioned log fire in the kitchen until thoroughly dried."

In his circular of July, 1900, Mr. H. P. Kelsey describes a good soil and the fundamental requirements of ginseng culture as follows: "The conditions of culture may be stated in a few words: A rich, cool, loamy, loose soil, shade, and a heavy mulching of wood leaves or similar covering in autumn, which is left on during the next summer to decay and conserve moisture. Ginseng will thrive in almost any rich garden soil if given shade, either natural or artificial, moisture and constant cultivation.

"This is the secret of growing ginseng, and although there are many ways of applying the above principles, still if these points are kept in view there can be but little doubt of success; where the conditions do not exist naturally, they can usually be artificially furnished.

"For those who intend planting on a large scale, the following suggestions will aid in making a proper start. First, where possible, select a cool, moist piece of ground, preferably level or nearly so, and where there is natural loam, or where the ground is loose and rich. Well-rotted stable manure is good for bringing up garden soil to a proper condition, as is also leaf-mold, rotted sods, etc. The ground must be fertile. Sandy soil, if rich and moist, is not objectionable, but rather desirable; but in any case the drainage must be good."

On another page Mr. Stanton makes some very important statements concerning the soil, statements the author wishes to strengthen as much as possible. No crop can be grown in continuous succession without gradually becoming poorer and becoming more subject to the attacks of enemies. A change of soil or a change of crop upon the soil is essential. In nature there is a rotation of crops; the lichens, those plants that live on rocks and tree trunks, are followed by mosses, mosses by ferns, ferns by flowering plants, among which there is a rotation also—pines often give place to scrub oak. Man has been slow to learn from nature, but he has learned this lesson from a master that he understands better—his pocketbook. It pays to practice rotation, and to supply humus.

Mr. Hart finds that humus may be easily supplied by muck. He writes in *Special Crops* in substance as follows:

"Although soils and locations varied greatly, in gardens where he used the largest proportion of muck the plants are thriving best, and from previous results he concludes that muck is one of the very best soils to add in preparing a bed for ginseng." He goes on to say that: "The cultivators will find that the soil is one of the most important features in cultivating this plant successfully. Of course the present cultivators are well aware of this, and the beginner will readily note how important it is that the soil should contain the elements essential to the growth of the plants. A good soil and a poor shade will bring larger returns than a poor soil and a perfect shade."

PREPARATION OF PERMANENT BEDS

It will be noticed that the growers all favor artificial shade and that the shade of trees (discussed on Page 23) is not now advised. Concerning the making of beds and shade Mr. Kelsey gives the following terse directions:

"The beds may be made either four or six feet wide, and any length, and should always be surrounded by boards firmly nailed to posts, giving a rest for the lath shades. The boards used are of ordinary inch boxing, and should extend two feet or more from the ground. Where six-feet-wide beds are made, the lath covers are made as shown in the illustration (Fig. 16); viz., four by six feet. Ordinary laths are nailed one inch apart to six-feet strips one inch thick and two inches wide, and then braced. Where the bed is made four feet wide, the laths are simply nailed to other laths with clinching nails. The latter size, being lighter, are the most easily handled covers, but the larger beds and shades are the most economical of room and lumber where the planting is on an extended scale. These lath covers are to stay on all summer, to be replaced by mulching and brush in winter. The beds and subsequent treatment after planting are the same for both seeds and plants."

TREATMENT OF SEEDLINGS

It is now generally believed that the distances recommended in the first part of this book for planting are too close. Roots two years old should be set not less than six inches apart and when four years old should be eight inches apart. If two-year-old roots are to remain for more than two years without transplanting, they should be given plenty of room at the start—eight inches. Mr. Kelsey's method of setting is quoted with the only comment that the distances are too small and that the planting board, as also the method of planting recommended by Mr. Fraser, are, in the author's opinion, less speedy and convenient than the method described and figured on Page 27.

"After the season's growth, the seedlings should be transplanted into permanent beds in the fall, after

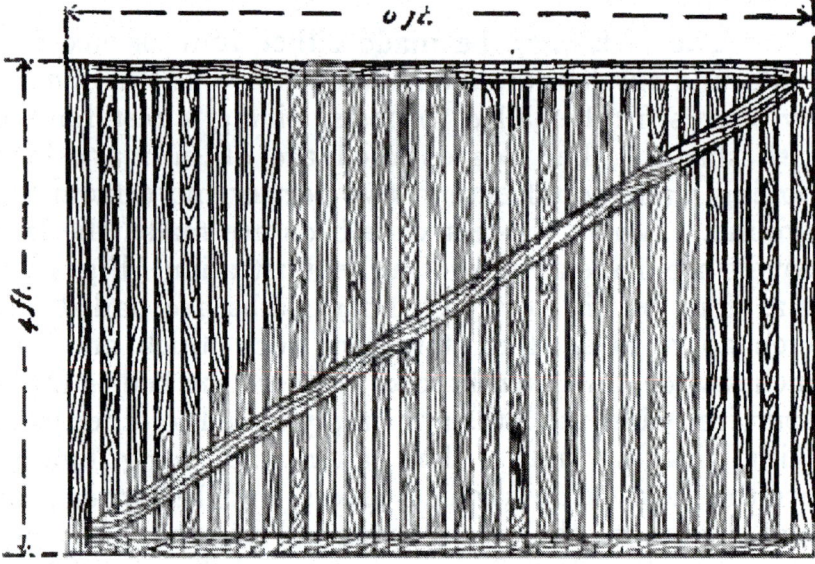

FIG 16. KELSEY'S LATH SHADE

the tops have died down. Some prefer to wait till the second autumn, but the roots are more liable to be injured, and it is very important that a good, clean tap root is preserved, making at maturity a larger and more salable article, that will command the best price.

"A planting board (Fig. 17) is made of three-quarter-inch white pine, or similar wood, five feet nine inches or three feet nine inches long, and one foot wide, to easily fit in the four-feet and six-feet beds. This board is braced by light strips tacked across the ends and middle to prevent warping, and notches five inches apart are cut on the edges. A trench is then opened, by using a light spade and lifting the soil away from the board, the back of the spade being flat against the edge of the board on which the planter is standing.

"The plants are set at the five-inch intervals, care being taken to see that the roots are in straight, and the crown at least an inch below the surface. Soil is pulled in with the hand as each plant is set, and after firming the row with the foot, the bed is smoothed off with a fine-toothed rake. The middle of the board is then placed directly over the row, and the planting of the next row is proceeded with. This leaves the plants five by six inches apart, each row containing fifteen plants in a six-feet-wide bed. To find out the number of plants such a bed will hold, multiply the length of the bed in feet by thirty.

"Some prefer sowing the seeds singly in drills two or three inches apart, and at intervals of one to two inches apart in the row. In this event the same planting board can be used, only the notches on one must be cut the required distance apart, the rows being three inches or less apart instead of six inches, as in the case of the plants. It is thus easy to figure out the area required for a given number of seeds."

Some growers, it will be observed, recommend the dibble in planting seedlings. There are serious objec-

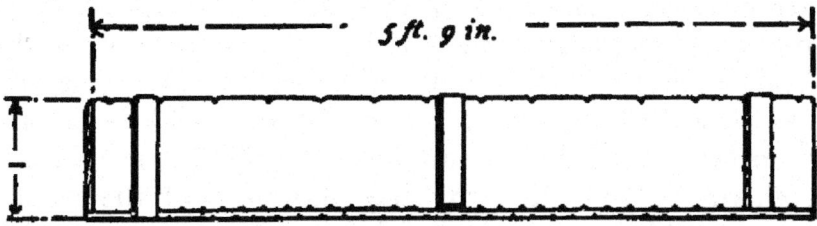

FIG 17. KELSEY'S PLANTING BOARD

tions to the use of this tool; first, it is apt to harden the soil close to the main root of the plant and thus make it difficult for the rootlets to penetrate; second, unless the tool be properly used the plant may be left suspended in a hole with no chance to strike root until the hardened walls of the hole cave in. The proper way to use this tool is to hang it up in the attic, unless the operator can trust himself to press the soil firmly around all sides of each plant that he sets. It seems necessary to repeat the statement that roots frequently transplanted will be straighter than those less often transplanted.

ARTIFICIAL PROPAGATION

With reference to artificial propagation (see Page 30) it seems that some growers have had poor success. Probably when seed becomes cheaper the methods will fall into disuse, but until that time it may be well to remember that neither a root without a crown nor a crown with only a small portion of root should be thrown away, but that each should be planted, because there is a chance that the missing part may be produced. Also, that some plants with roots that meet at a common point, like that illustrated on Page 12, may be divided with fair chances of obtaining additional plants.

MANURING

Several writers speak of "enriching" the soil. But by this they do not mean loading the soil with fresh stable manure, nitrate of soda and all sorts of nitrogenous plant food. This practice would fill the heart with gladness to look at the leaves and stems, but the production of root and of seed would be disappointing. No, they mean *improve the texture* of the soil, make the soil light like the loam of the woods where wild flowers grow. You eat some sugar each day, but what good would you be if your diet consisted of nothing but sugar? Balance up, friend. Give fresh ashes, bone meal and other fertilizers containing potash and phosphoric acid. They will give vigor.

The decay of the humus you add should supply all the nitrogen necessary. If not, it may easily be added in the form of manure, or nitrate of soda.

ENEMIES

Since the preparation of the first edition, no new or specially troublesome enemies have appeared in the ginseng plantations. Slugs and snails have caused some damage, but it is believed they may be combated without danger to the plants by sprinkling finely powdered fresh quicklime upon both plants and beds as soon as these creatures arrive. It tends to dry up the animals and thus destroy them. Snails and slugs are generally most active during the night, and should their presence be suspected, the grower should come out after dark to make inspection. The lime is not a poison and will not do the soil any harm but, if applied in reasonable quantities, rather good.

Mr. Stanton calls special attention to nematode worms which attack the roots. These pests may be expected in any plantation, but fortunately they have not spread very generally as yet. No satisfactory remedy has been suggested; the only practices as yet tried are heating the soil, or freezing it.

Concerning the most important enemies of ginseng—men, mice and moles—Mr. Sears and Mr. Kelsey make the following statements:

"Moles must be kept out. The best way to get rid of them is to watch for them and when one of them is observed moving the soil, quickly step in behind it, dig it out and destroy it. We have a ground mouse with a short tail like that of the mole; they eat the roots. The only remedy I know for them is poisoned bait. I soak a few grains of corn in water with strychnine, drop in their burrows; they follow in the burrows made by the mole, or work along just beneath the leaves on the beds in the loose soil, and begin to eat on the top of the roots. We have but few of them, two or three are all that have ever given me any trouble. Then we have what is called field or woods mice; they eat the seeds from the seed head while the berries are ripening; they do not eat the seeds after they are planted. Before the berries begin to ripen, I set a few deadfalls, and in a few nights I have cleared away the mice. I have noticed a little white fly that sometimes gets on the stem of some of the plants, near the seed head; they can be removed quickly with the thumb and finger. If allowed to remain on the stem they will cause it to perish. I sometimes sprinkle ashes lightly on the growing plants; this I think is a good preventive. We have here what is called a ginseng cricket; it is of a green color. They are very easily caught with the hand and destroyed. This green cricket cuts into the kernel of the ginseng seed and eats it before the berry gets ripe, while green. In my nursery I have but few, if any, of these pests to contend with; they give me but little trouble. Chickens, pigs, etc, must be strictly kept out; it will not do to let them in at all. The ginseng beds should be inclosed with a strong slat fence."

"Unless secrecy can be maintained it will pay, as a rule, to erect a high, solid wall with barbed wire on top. An electric wire can be arranged around the plantation at little cost, which will ring a bell or bells, located where desired, if an entry be forced Any very valuable article finds ready thieves, if unprotected— ginseng being no exception to the rule— but it is amply worth any expense incurred in protecting it."

Diseases have been hinted at as causing trouble in some places, but none, so far as the author can learn, have been identified. Since they are probably of a fungous nature, however, and also probably carried from plant to plant by snails, slugs and insects, *prevention of infection* is the watchword. Prevent infection by keeping the snails, etc., in check and prevent disease from gaining entrance by spraying with Bordeaux mixture or some other fungicide. If the fungicide be properly prepared and applied, it should be efficacious The method of making Bordeaux mixture is as follows:

1. Put twenty-five gallons of water in a wooden or crockery vessel (not a metal one) and hang five pounds of copper sulphate (blue stone) contained in a cloth bag in the water, so that the bottom of the bag is slightly below the surface of the water. This is the quickest way to dissolve the sulphate. Don't dump the sulphate in so that it goes to the bottom, because this is the slowest way of all to get it dissolved.

2. In another vessel, slake four pounds of the freshest and best stone or shell lime, using only a little water until the lime is dissolved. Strain the liquid through fine burlap or coarse cloth and dilute with water until the total quantity of water present is twenty-five gallons.

3. These two liquids may be mixed in the proportion of gallon for gallon, the lime solution being stirred before mixing, and both thoroughly stirred while being mixed together. While being applied they should be kept stirred up to prevent settling. The shorter the time between the time of slaking the lime and the mixing with the sulphate, and also the shorter the time between the mixing of the two solutions and applying to plants, the better, because the particles will not have much chance to become large and hard. The finer the particles, the better.

4. When applied to plants the finest nozzle obtainable must be used. The Vermorel is perhaps the best.

5. Now, make no mistake: this spray must be a *spray*, not a dribble, nor a drizzle, nor a squirt, but a *mist*. It must look like a little fog at the end of the hose and must reach every part of the plant, partic-

ularly the undersides of the leaves, mind, just enough so it won't trickle off. And this must be applied as soon as the first sign of disease is seen. It will also be good to thoroughly spray all posts, walks, etc., to kill disease germs that may be resting upon them.

Let no grower be surprised at the appearance of diseases. He is largely responsible for them because he has taken the plant from its natural surroundings and is making it grow under artificial conditions. It may be that he is giving too much shade, too little air, too much nitrogen, that the plants are too crowded, the soil too moist—whatever the wrong condition, he must find out and correct it. It is safe to say that the grower who most nearly approaches natural conditions will be least troubled with disease. Keep the plants healthy by rational feeding, which will tend to make them strong and to keep them so, then by careful spraying, prevent the entrance of disease. Just think of a ginseng disease as ginseng cancer. When cancer gets a start there is no cure. Spraying is not a remedy, it is a preventive; it is an insurance.

SELECTION FOR IMPROVEMENT

The author is especially pleased to note the interest that is being taken in the selection of ginseng to obtain improved varieties. Not that any marked improvements such as those mentioned on Pages 37-39 have been made, but that the more progressive growers are making observations and drawing deductions.

Since the writing of Part I the most important discovery perhaps of all in connection with ginseng, is the fact that the seeds of some plants and the earliest ripened seeds of others do not always wait until the second spring to germinate, but sprout during the first spring, thus saving a whole year's time. When a plant shows a tendency to hustle like this no grower should lose an opportunity to help it.

This early maturing trait should be taken advantage of as a starting. In fact some enterprising growers are already planning to develop varieties that will always sprout during the spring following the ripening of the seed. Such improved varieties should be named and disseminated. There is not the slightest reason to doubt that ginseng can be improved by selection and cultivation, in similar manner as has been done with carrots, beets, parsnips and many other cultivated crops that have been developed from the original wild forms.

The statements made upon this subject in the first part are hereby emphasized. But neither the author's talking nor the grower's wondering about them will accomplish anything. The way to prove the truth of the assertions is to test them. Turn to Page 38, read and think this matter over again, remembering during the perusal that when the prices of seeds and plants fall—as fall they must—the man who has a good variety, a variety worthy of a name, may still command a high price—perhaps not so high as at present is asked —yet not so high that his conscience will trouble him for accepting it, because he will be giving a superior article for the money. There is no reason why varieties noted for early sprouting, early maturing, long straight heavy roots, ability to withstand disease better than common stock, etc., etc., should not be advertised within the next ten years in the same way that seedsmen advertise early and late, green and yellow podded, black and white seeded beans The whole matter rests with the grower. He should first make himself thoroughly familiar with the plant and its peculiarities Then, for reasons already detailed, he should start his improvements with the best stock obtainable.

Considerable as have been the improvements made in the growing of ginseng, which twenty years ago was not in cultivation in America, the author believes and confidently predicts that as great discoveries are to be made and improvements wrought in the business as have been recorded and attained up to the present time.

In this connection it may be said that a well conducted organization of ginseng growers and dealers should be of great benefit to the industry, since methods of selecting, cultivating, harvesting, drying, packing and marketing, and other matters pertinent to the ginseng business could be freely discussed. Mr. E. C. Robertson, of Dickson, Tenn., who seems to be the first to propose such an organization, writes in the July issue (1902) of *Special Crops* concerning this matter as follows:

"There is one thing which I should like to see effected, and that right soon—an organization of ginseng growers Now is the time to start such an organization while the industry is in its infancy and the planters are comparatively few. With the right kind of officers, the ginseng growers need have no fears about future prices, for the association can control the supply, and thereby the prices. Besides, such a movement will do away with many of the objectionable features of handling the marketable roots in this country. It is one of the most important things for consideration at this time, and I suggest an early meeting of all who are interested in the growing of ginseng . . . for the perfection of plans and the completion of such an organization as may be desired. After the national meeting, the several states can organize, and then work in harmony for the benefit of the cause."

Mr. Sears publishes a recent letter from Wells & Co. concerning the improvement in general market ginseng. The letter reads as follows: "The improvement in ginseng is most conspicuously shown in southern root, i. e., root grown south of the Ohio river. This is for two reasons: wild root from the South is smaller in size and more pithy in substance than northern root. Under cultivation, our observations so far have been that the root is increased almost to the size of the northern cultivated root. However, the northern root is much smoother on the surface and we think somewhat whiter. This last item, color, is influenced somewhat by the soil. Proportionately, southern root shows a greater improvement under cultivation than the northern; this is partly due to the inferior quality of the wild root. We think it can be still further improved and that it will be further improved, as it takes some time to change the characteristics of the plant."

CULTIVATED VERSUS WILD ROOT

Comparing the statements of dealers and growers one with another and with those of the consuls, it will be seen that the claims made for cultivated root in Part I (Page 40) are being realized in the small quantities of cultivated ginseng that are being marketed. The statements which the author made in the place referred to seem to need no revision, since the qualities—size, weight, form and smoothness—are found more frequently in garden ginseng than in wild. The cultivated plants have other advantages of which Mr. Sears speaks as follows:

"In November, 1900, I took from my nursery fifty six-year-old, cultivated roots from the seeds; their weight, green, was eight pounds; dried, three and one-sixteenth pounds, and sold for a fraction over thirty-six cents each. It will be remembered that these roots produced a fine crop of seed each year after the first. The two best roots together weighed eight ounces, green; when dried one weighed one and one-half ounces, the other, one and three-fourths. The two roots together sold for a fraction over $1.21."

With respect to cultivated versus wild roots, Mr. Hart says: "As an illustration—the wild roots, in general, collected from the forests, will average an age of from eight to twenty years, and it is seldom that the cultivator will find these roots as large as the general run of cultivated roots when they are three years old. Now, by planting these wild roots, they will, as a rule, bear from ten to twenty seeds to the plant, and, after being planted for two years, may attain a weight of from two and one-half to three ounces, green—while the cultivated roots, under favorable conditions, should bear from sixty to eighty seeds to the plant the fourth year, and from one hundred to one hundred and twenty-five thereafter, and will attain a weight of from four to five ounces, green, at five years old. Now, I do not wish my readers to think that an entire garden of ginseng will bear this amount of seed each season, for every plant does not bear seed every year, and in digging up a garden, while a majority of the plants will have attained this large development, a portion of them must be graded out and replanted; not that they are not marketable, but because it is more profitable to let them remain for another season or two."

In general, the case of cultivated ginseng seems to be won, but there are little points that must not be overlooked; namely, there is likely to be an overstimulation of seed production as long as high prices persist (see letters from Messrs. Eisenhauer, Wells and Stanton) which will tend to impair root development; the product of different growers is likely to be variable until definite methods of growing are agreed upon and definite grades of product made; the cultivated roots are likely to lack a flavor that the wild root possesses (see letter from Messrs. Eisenhauer & Co.) or, what amounts to the same thing, to possess a flavor that the wild root lacks, so that the final purchaser may not fancy it. Now is the time, therefore, to establish control of the plant and to make it meet the oriental requirements.

In this connection several hints are furnished by the consuls, and others by Mr. T. B. Cunningham, of Baltimore, Md., who has spent several years in Hong Kong, being connected with the exporting trade, and who is enthusiastic over the cultivation of ginseng in America. Mr. Cunningham stated, during an interview with Mr. Hart, "that he did not believe too much pains could be taken in perfecting the American article to the highest standard, in order to maintain the great demand for the American root in China. Therefore, it seems prudent for the present cultivators to exercise the greatest care in cultivating, preparing for market and marketing this product, knowing that the Chinese are very cautious in their dealings, and that it would be much easier to depreciate the market with inferior quality roots than it would be to regain the confidence of the Chinese after such harm had been done."

It seems only necessary to add that the production of a good quality of root is not the last stage; there is yet the marketing, which, at present, is far too carelessly performed. If the reader feel a doubt as to this, let him look in the nearest grocery store at the packages of breakfast foods. These products are made from the same grains as the now unsalable, old-fashioned oatmeal and graham flour of our grandfathers' days. The principal reason that the new materials sell and the old do not, is that the former please the eye— "they look good." In the sale of ginseng the case is the same. The Chinese customer is like the American customer; he won't hunt all over town to find the dirtiest ginseng he can get, and then force a high price upon the dealer as a premium for dirtiness. The Chinese appreciate cleanliness, neatness and attractiveness more than they are supposed to. Neat, clean boxes lined with clean paper and filled with clean, unbroken roots will attract customers who will be willing to pay advanced prices for articles that look well.

CLARIFICATION. 75

Since nothing is mentioned in the first edition concerning clarification, and since there seems to be a growing interest in the process and the product, the following paragraphs are quoted from Bulletin 16 of the Division of Botany:

"A process employed by the Chinese to produce a yellowish translucent appearance in the ginseng root, which adds to its value in their estimation, is thus described by Father Jartoux:

"'They take care to wash it well and cleanse it with a brush from all extraneous matter. Then they dip it into scalding water, and prepare it in the fume of a sort of yellow millet, which communicates to it a part of its color. The millet is put into a vessel with a little water, and boils over a gentle fire; the roots are laid upon small transverse pieces of wood over the vessel, and are thus prepared, being covered with a linen cloth or some other vessel placed over them. They may also be dried in the sun or by the fire; but then, though they retain their virtue well enough, yet they have not that yellow color which the Chinese so much admire. When the roots are dried, they must be kept close in some very dry place; otherwise they are in danger of corrupting or being eaten by worms.'

"Another authority, referring apparently to the same Chinese custom, states: 'It is cured by steaming in a steaming basket. If intended for use in the South, sugar is added; if for use in the North, no sugar.'

"The clarifying process is thus described by Mr. Foulk: 'Soon after the seeds have been gathered in October the plants and roots intact are carefully taken from the earth. The stems are readily broken off, the roots washed, placed in small baskets with large meshes, and at once taken to the steaming house. Here are flat, shallow iron boilers over fireplaces, over which are earthenware vessels, two feet in diameter and as many high, with close-fitting lids. In the bottoms of the earthenware vessels are five holes two inches in diameter. Water is boiled in the iron vessels, the steam rising and filling the upper vessels through these holes.

" 'The small baskets containing the roots having been placed in the earthen vessel and the latter tightly closed, the steaming process goes on for from one and a half to four hours, when the roots are removed and taken to the drying house. This is a long building containing racks of bamboo poles, on which in rows are placed flat drying baskets. Under the floor of the house, at intervals of three or four feet, are fireplaces, the smoke from which passes out of small holes in the back of the house under the floor level. In the baskets of the drying house the roots are spread and the fires kept going constantly for about ten days, when the roots are supposed to be cured. From here they are packed for the market in rectangular willow baskets closely lined with paper to exclude moisture

" 'During this process the roots become very toughly hard, and their color changes from carroty white to nearly a cherrywood red. They break hard but crisply, exhibiting a shiny, glassy fracture, translucent, dark red. The ginseng resulting from this process is called *hong-sam* (red ginseng), and is the article prohibited from export from Korea in all the treaties made by Korea with the western powers. It is the most common ginseng seen in Korea and by far the majority of it is produced in the Songto section.'

"The treatment last described is doubtless that which is most properly called 'clarification,' since specimens purchased in Korea, through the Department of State, and now in the pharmacological collection of the Division of Botany, answer the description given by Mr. Foulk. Similar specimens were also seen in Mr. Stanton's museum. Doubtless American skill can produce an article by some such method which would be acceptable to the Chinese, but it would hardly be wise to undertake steaming on a large scale without fuller information or careful experiment."

Messrs. A. C. Hartzell & Co., Addison, Pa., describe their method as follows: "Wash the roots nice and clean, put water in some kind of a boiler or kettle, put the ginseng in a sack and place in the kettle, cover so as to keep in the steam, being careful not to let the ginseng get in the water. Steam for three to four hours, or until soft; take out and dry. The ginseng must be green and not over a week old, and if kept a week it should be damp so it does not start to dry, as this will not make nice, clear ginseng. We have handled thousands of pounds in this way, clarifying some years as much as fifteen to twenty thousands green."

PROFITS

The author believes that the evidence presented in the section "Profits" in Part I is so strong in itself that he need say little. It will doubtless be matter for surprise to most readers to learn the facts contained in the first letter quoted: namely, that Canada has no export trade in ginseng. By referring to Page 3 it will be seen that nearly two hundred years have elapsed since American ginseng was discovered, and that the discovery was made near Montreal, Canada. The price paid for exported Canadian root rose to more than five dollars a pound, but now the Canadian article is unknown in China. Whether the injury done in 1752 by the shipment of inferior root is so well remembered by the Chinese merchants that they no longer call for Canadian ginseng, but rather shun it, or whether the root in Canada is actually becoming extinct, the author cannot say. He inclines to the latter view. He can say, however, that the openings for a profitable industry in Canada are excellent. It may be that direct exportation might not be favored by the Chinese and that the Canadian product would have to reach China as American root. But even so, neither the Canadian exporter nor his product should suffer. Turn about is fair play; certain American products are sent abroad from Canadian ports as Canadian!

The letter referred to above was written to Mr. James Fletcher, Botanist of the Dominion Experimental Farm, by Mr. George Johnson, Statistician of the Canadian Department of Agriculture at Ottawa, Ontario, Canada. "I have to say that Canada is an importer to a small extent of ginseng, and my belief is that it is pretty well run out. At any rate our trade returns do not indicate that we exported any in recent years. Possibly there is a small quantity exported, but not likely. My recollection, so far as Canada is concerned, is that we produced quite a quantity at one time and that it was very good. It would be, I should think, worth while if the Experimental Farms would inquire into the causes of the abandonment of the ginseng trade in Canada. It certainly was not because the quality was poor, because China thought well of it, and it was not because the supply was greater than the demand, as for some years back there has been a tendency to an increase in the price. We ought certainly to have a good trade in ginseng with China."

In proof that the American supply of wild ginseng is declining, the statements made on Page 13 and the table of exports on Page 47 find additional support in the following letter from Messrs. A. C. Hartzell & Co.:

"We have been in the ginseng business for over fifty years, and have bought as much as 130,000 pounds in one season, but of course, that was some years ago; and we have in fifty years handled close to the million mark. We have in times past bought as much as 5000 pounds from one party, and in a season we would find quite a few who would have that much; but if you were to go to the same places now you would not find possibly more than from five to fifty pounds, and at some of them you would not find the five."

These statements are also upheld by the following export figures for the four years that have passed since the appearance of Part I of this book. These figures form a continuation of the table given on Page 47, and are derived from the same source; viz, the Bureau of Statistics of the United States Treasury Department. The great increase in the average price per pound cannot fail to strike even the casual reader

Year	Pounds	Valued at	Average per pound
1899	196,196	$782,545	$4 00
1900	160,901	833,710	5 18
1901	149,069	801,672	5.31
1902	154,063	856,515	5.55

The author is indebted to the several firms whose names appear below for prices paid by them to collectors and growers. Messrs. Samuel Wells & Co., Cincinnati, Ohio, whose list of prices for the years 1889-1898 is given on Page 47, quote the following for the last three years:

Year	Fair	Choice
1899	$2.50-4 90	$3.50-7.25
1900	3.50-4.75	4.00-6.10
1901	3.75-5.25	4.50-7.25

In November, 1901, the same firm addressed the following communication to Orange Judd Company:

"We have paid for the best qualities of cultivated root in 1899 somewhat over $8, 1900—$7, and this year on an average of about the same price as last. We consider cultivated ginseng worth about twenty per cent more than the wild; however, this is a very difficult matter to determine exactly, as the value of each lot of cultivated root depends entirely upon the grower. Some men with greater intelligence than others produce much more satisfactory results."

Messrs. J. L. Prouty, of New York city, under date of December 6, 1901, wrote to Orange Judd Company as follows:

"Northern ginseng root this season has sold from $6 to $7 per pound as to size, etc. Southern root from $4.50 to $5.50 per pound, clean and off strings. These prices have been fully seventy-five cents to $1 per pound higher than season of 1900. As to the cultivated ginseng root no quantities this year have been put upon the market to establish separate prices, still we have sold a few small lots of the cultivated at $7 50 and $8 per pound, grown in New York State. The cultivated root has a different taste and a certain character which we can distinguish from the wild, crude root and should some of the growers clarify this root 'twould sell for at least $10 per pound."

Mr. T. A. Bronson in November, 1901, quotes the following:

Ginseng, fair to choice, wild dug,
	1899	$5.00 to $6 50
	1900	$5 00 to $6.50
	1901	$5.75 to $7 00

Ginseng, cultivated, *choice* sold this year, $9, ordinary $7.50 to $8 Specially good lots wild dug may have commanded $7.50, but this was exceptional.

Dealers in the South were unknown to the author when the first edition was prepared, but two have been found who have furnished their prices. Messrs. Wallace Bros., Statesville, N. C., wrote as follows on July 25, 1902: "From September to January, 1900, we paid for ginseng root, wild, $4 per pound, for cultivated, $4.50. And during the season of 1900 we paid $4.50 and $5 respectively. A number of parties are cultivating ginseng in this section, but supplies to date have not been large."

Messrs. Speyer & Son, Lexington, Ky., had this to say on July 22, 1902: "We are now paying from $3.25 to $3.50 per pound for Kentucky ginseng; cultivated root will bring from $4.25 to $4.50. The cultivation of ginseng is becoming more common each year, and of course the more it is cultivated the cheaper it will be. The market to-day is extremely dull, with a lower tendency."

Messrs. Eisenhauer & Co., under date of July 23, 1902, wrote as follows: "Our prices for fall dug ginseng last season in average lots, ranged from about $4 for small fibery roots from Kentucky and Tennessee to about $7 for 'seng from the best sections—this, when our market was at its strongest. The quantity of ginseng cultivated and marketed, thus far, is quite insignificant, although considering the number of persons now interested in its culture, there ought to be a material improvement in this respect during the next year or two. The fact that shipments of cultivated root consist chiefly of large selected pieces (the smaller specimens being put back into the ground) means of course that it has been bringing higher prices than average lots of wild roots. Otherwise it is of no greater value, and we have been informed by consumers that it lacks somewhat the peculiar flavor possessed by the wild growing 'seng, which will hurt its value should it ever be exported in noteworthy quantities.

"The outlook this season is not at all satisfactory. The unusually low value of silver, together with a light demand in Hong Kong, has caused losses to the exporters on a large proportion of their purchases, and in some cases these losses were quite severe. If you will consider the extraordinary advance in ginseng during the past few years—to a large extent forced and unnatural—and the continued depression in silver during the same period, you will realize somewhat the steep advance in price the Chinese consumers had to submit to. A reaction is bound to occur, and it looks as though it has already set in. At any rate, if exporters are to make any profit on their purchases this season, they will have to be far more conservative than during the past two or three years. Many publications are going the rounds in which the idea is conveyed that there is no limit to the price which the Chinese will pay for ginseng, but this is all nonsense, and only deceives the farmer into buying a lot of seeds, etc., for the doubtful cultivating venture."

A similar set of ideas is held by Messrs. Wells & Co., who on July 17, 1902, had the following to say: "Of recent years the prices of ginseng have been advanced by gamblers and speculators through the country very materially, at the same time the crop has been practically the same annually and the consumption diminishing owing to the advancing prices and the growing troubles in the consuming market in China. This has culminated in the conditions existing to-day: viz., at the beginning of this season, practically one-half of last season's crop was still unsold in the hands of exporters and some large dealers who have a speculative trend; heavy losses that have been sustained on all goods sold; a very much reduced consuming market, because of the poverty of the consumer and inability to pay the high prices demanded; serious military and mercantile disturbances in China, which have resulted in almost a total closing of the market; and the complete disregard of the financial side of the business; viz., the course of bullion silver by all large dealers this season. In the face of all this, handlers through the country are paying and demanding approximately last season's prices; this will result in loss to someone.

"Cultivated ginseng, because of the very small quantity harvested and the superior quality of the root, is influenced less by the depressing conditions probably than the wild article, although it feels to a large extent the depression. It is to be hoped that the price of ginseng can be kept down lower than the prices of last year, as unless this be done the article will still be beyond the reach of the masses and we will be bothered by an overstocked market continually.

"Some years ago some brokers in this country imported considerable Japanese ginseng, which in appearance is very similar to the American article, and before the trade in this country knew it, had disposed of fifteen-cent root for mixing with American ginseng, which was then worth from $2.50 to $4.50, according to its quality. When discovered by the Chinese in Hong Kong it nearly ruined the business of every exporter in whose shipments this Japanese ginseng was found, and the innocent exporter in this country suffered severely, while for some years the American ginseng business was considerably affected. Of late, either under misrepresentation or through unscrupulousness, some American dealers in settings for gardens have been advertising and pushing Japanese seed, claiming in their advertisements that it is almost as good as the American article and will be highly profitable to the cultivator. Commercially Japanese ginseng is practically worthless, and will kill the cultivating of American ginseng in this country if permitted to get a foothold in our gardens. The danger of handling Japanese ginseng cannot be too forcibly impressed upon the trade and the grower, and we can only say for ourselves that, knowing a man to be raising Japanese root, we will do everything in our power to injure his business, as it would be a protection not only to ourselves but to the entire trade to have the Japanese article stamped out completely."

On July 21, 1902, the same firm wrote Mr. Sears as follows: "You have asked us in the past in regard to overstocking the market with cultivated ginseng. We do not think it is possible to overstock the market, for many reasons:

"First. The article is of such a slow growth that it will take many years before the American gardens can produce a sufficient quantity to supply the normal demand.

"Second. As the crop increases in volume, it naturally should decrease somewhat in price, and this will restrain many from going into the business.

"Third. As the price declines, making it possible to sell at a lower figure in China, the consuming market in China will increase, making a consumption of a greater quantity of root possible.

"For several years past the production of American wild ginseng has been about stationary, at from about 125,000 to 130,000 pounds per annum. In this same period prices have advanced fully one hundred per cent, with the result that the price has gone out of reach of the vast majority of Chinamen who formerly used ginseng, and it is now used only by the select few. Consequently when the season opened this year, exporters carried over from last season's goods more than one-half the crop, or based upon the sales made in China last year, more than a year's supply. All this could be sold in a hurry if prices were sufficiently low. However, there is always a demand for ginseng, although if a sufficient volume of cultivated root were offered the price on the wild would be very low, probably one-half of that for cultivated root. We do not know what this price for cultivated root should be, as no two gardens develop exactly the same quality of ginseng, and as no two cultivators pay the same attention to their plants. There eventually will be a standard by which all gardens will work, but until that is reached there will be no uniform price that will be of advantage for anyone to know. We have paid as high as $10 per pound for cultivated ginseng in the past, but under the conditions existing to-day, would not pay that. However, we cannot positively state now what similar root to this would be worth, but it will be worth considerably more than the wild at any time."

The statements made in the last three letters may, at first sight, appear to be not very encouraging to the would-be, or to the actual ginseng grower. The author hereby admits that he was surprised at the state of affairs, but after considering the matter in a calm, unbiased way, which, being neither a grower of nor dealer in ginseng, he believes himself able to do, he ventures to express the opinion that altogether the signs are hopeful. Let him obtrude his reasons.

First. Ginseng is not a staple crop, like wheat, rice, potatoes or apples, which mankind would find inconvenience in doing without. It is at best a condiment used to give "meat a flavor the Chinese people like." In no household, therefore, can it compare in the expense account with even the least frequently used food. And in consequence its consumption must decline as the income of the family decreases, or, what amounts to the same thing, as its price increases. In short, as soon as the family can no longer afford ginseng it will cease to be purchased. Its greatest consumption, however, is not as a luxury but as a drug, and as such, no matter how important it may be or may become, it can never rise to the dignity of a staple. The food products, products used to clothe and to shelter the body—in a word—necessities must always outclass it.

Second. Its rank, present and prospective, having been proved, its standing in the market must be investigated. Legitimately, the price of any article is based upon the law of supply and demand. The price may rise because the demand exceeds the supply; this is determined by the market. It may rise also, because, for reasons beyond the control of the market, the cost of production is increased. It may fall because the consumption declines and the marketman, who in order to save himself from loss of interest, or of principal, or of both, is willing to make a slight sacrifice, lowers the price so as to reach a class of customers less able to pay the customary price than his regular patrons. It may also fall because the producer has cheapened his processes, or has a large quantity upon which he is willing to make only a small profit. Every item of evidence points to the fact that the supply of American ginseng is decreasing; therefore, the difficulty and consequently the expense of obtaining the root are growing greater each year. Under such conditions an increased price must result, and has resulted. On the other hand, the demand for ginseng is decreasing because, being a luxury and a drug, people of small means find they cannot afford to purchase it.

Third. The case thus far detailed is fair and should cause no complaint on the part of either seller or buyer, but, regardless of the reduced demand and the legitimately high price caused by lessened supply, the price is forced higher still, and the market, already threatened, shows signs of paralysis, which when it occurs will be followed by a considerable reduction in prices and a consequent sale, "in a hurry," of the supply of ginseng on hand.

Fourth. A period of readjustment must follow and the industry must assume a more healthy form. With the crash, and with the decline in price, the hunters of the wild root, who already find difficulty in obtaining a supply, will become discouraged and very many of them will stop collecting the root. This will, of course, reduce the quantity of wild root exported, and the demand, which will have been stimulated by the increased consumption of cheapened root now, or soon to be upon the market, will increase and will warrant an advance in price. At this juncture, the grower who has been quietly extending his beds will have a chance.

Finally. At the risk of inviting severe censure from growers who sell seeds and roots for planting, the author feels called upon to state his belief that the establishment of the ginseng industry in America will be hastened if every grower and dealer will exert his utmost influence to prevent the recurrence of such exorbitant prices as have been recorded in the last few years. Further, he believes that the grower who will put in practice the methods suggested for the origination of improved ginseng varieties; who will cultivate his plants for their roots and not for the sake of the money their seed will bring, who will give adequate attention to the needs of his plants from sowing to digging; and who will place upon the market dried roots that he can take honest pride in because of their prime quality—such a grower should have no reason to complain of his income, even though the price he receive be lower than the lowest annual export average price per pound during the last ten years.

These assertions as to the advisability of a reduction of price and to the profit to be derived at such price, are bold and broad; but while the author wishes to call attention to the fact that no estimates of what may be made in ginseng culture properly so called, i. e., for the dried root, in a given space of time have been quoted or inserted in his book, yet he feels sure that, properly managed, and even at the low figure referred to, the growing of ginseng should yield a profit that should compare favorably with the profit made upon any of our farm, garden or orchard crops.

Before concluding this section special attention must be called to what has been said about Japanese ginseng, concerning which the reader should turn up the references given in the index. Every item possible has been collected concerning this root; not a single one is in favor of it. If a warning be worth anything to the individual grower, the author feels it his duty to say very clearly and emphatically: *leave Japanese ginseng alone;* and to the dealer: *do all in your power to check the growing of this root.* The individual will be injured by it, but more important, the ginseng industry in America will be put in jeopardy.

ADULTERATION AND FRAUD

The following quotation from the Somerset (Ky.) *Journal* of October 19, 1900, and a similar thought in Mr. Stanton's letters, meet the view of all prominent growers of ginseng: "In our investigations of the business of 'sang' culture, one thing especially impresses the writer, and that is that while the opportunities for fraud and fake are golden, there is not the slightest reason why a cultivator of the plant or a seller of his product should ever resort to any sort of misrepresentation or fraud to profit in the business, as it is amply remunerative without the aid of trickery of any kind."

But trickery is resorted to, and also statements of a too lurid character. Concerning the adulteration of the dried root the following extract from Bulletin 16 is given:

"In the sale of ginseng in China various frauds are perpetrated, consisting of the mixture of lower grades with the higher and the substitution of other kinds of roots. The Korean root, which ranks after the Manchurian, constitutes the only available supply of native root in the hands of traders. This root is frequently sophisticated; Japanese ginseng, which is itself often adulterated with the roots of *Campanula glauca,* being often found mixed with it. Other species of Campanulaceae belonging to the genera Adenophora and Platycodon are frequently used to adulterate and replace the genuine root, and it has even been stated that Japanese ginger has been found in some samples.

"It has been claimed by Messrs. Hirsch & Lowenstein, of New York, that Japanese ginseng has been imported into the United States, shipped to the interior of the ginseng country, sold to country merchants in small quantities, and resold by them to the wholesalers, who export it as American ginseng. Upon learning of this alleged fraud, authentic specimens of American and Japanese root, the latter imported by the Department of Agriculture from Japan, were examined by Mr. A. J. Pieters of the Division of Botany. He found upon careful microscopical study of cross and longitudinal sections that no characters can be found in the Japanese roots which are not also observed in the American. It is stated by one ginseng dealer that when the Japanese root is broken in two the surfaces of the fracture differ from similar surfaces in broken American root in much the same way that the fractured surfaces of the hard wheats differ from similar surfaces in the soft wheats. It has been noticed, however, that some specimens of American root have the same kind of fracture as the Japanese, and the difference may be merely an incidental variation due to different methods in drying; roots dried in mild heat exposing a different fracture from roots dried more quickly in a more intense heat. This test is, however, not sufficiently constant to be of general application.

"Unless Japanese ginseng could be laid down in New York in wholesale quantities by sailing vessels it would cost too much to distribute the root in small lots to the country dealers for mixing and reshipment. If it were imported in any considerable quantity, it seems more likely that the adulteration would be practiced in the New York market by the wholesalers themselves.

It is believed, however, that no adulteration with the Japanese article worthy of extended notice is practiced, since the imports of Japanese ginseng into the United States for the years 1895 and 1896 were $846.60 and $358.19 respectively. Even if the whole of this imported ginseng were used for sophistication of American roots, it would form but a very small percentage of the actual output, which amounted in 1896 to $770,673; but it is believed that this Japanese root found its way to the States upon the Pacific Coast, there to be used not to adulterate the American article, but to supply the demand of the resident Chinese and Japanese.

"Apart from adulteration there is little fraud practiced, except by a few collectors, who load the root with nails, screws, lead, and other heavy substances to make the sample 'weigh up well.' These foreign substances may be inserted while the root is soft with comparative ease. Upon drying, the shrinking of the root generally exposes the metal. Little loss is sustained, however, through this fraud, since the wholesaler refuses such roots as have been plugged, and the country merchant is supposed to shift his prices when bartering groceries and dry goods for ginseng roots."

Perhaps, however, more disappointment is caused by misrepresentation of the possibilities of ginseng culture in a short time upon any kind of soil from muck to brick clay, than by any other kind of fraud. Exaggerated statements based upon estimates are common in the daily papers, and it is believed that many would-be ginseng growers are duped annually in consequence. As a matter of fact careful authorities are of opinion that the present area devoted to ginseng that will be ready for market within the next two years is probably less than ten acres. And this is largely in plats of only a few square rods at most, and the largest part of which, so far as the grower of it is concerned, will be the first crop dug. In general, therefore, the statements as to amounts that can be obtained from acres are misleading. There are very few men who have sold dried root from more than a square rod at a time, and who can give an accurate account of the cost of production from even that small area.

These estimates recall the statement made by a certain prominent man as to the rate potatoes could be dug with a power potato digger. The author can vouch for the facts in the case, which were as follows: In a level field where the soil was free from obstructions, a pair of horses, better and stronger than most farm horses, was made to haul the digger as quickly as possible once across the field, a distance of about one hundred yards, account being taken of the time. From this the time necessary to dig an acre was calculated, no account being taken of the time necessary to turn the team to start back on the next row. The rate was announced as a possible one. In practice, it is doubtful if any team could have worked day in day out and made half the speed even upon most favorable land. The statement was not fair to the machine, to the horses, nor to the man who made it

The paragraph quoted below from *Special Crops* shows the way in which similar estimates are made in ginseng culture. This, it will be noticed, is for the seed, but numerous similar estimates are published concerning the root. "We know that there are extravagant claims made about the profits to be reaped in the cultivation of ginseng. Facts are facts—and when we see right before our eyes what is being accomplished, we feel like saying to certain editors of agricultural papers that they should go a little slow about charging falsehood and misrepresentation upon ginseng growers. Our best plant last year gave us one hundred and seventeen seeds. That plant was in a bed, where plants were set six inches apart each way. These seeds were sold for a penny apiece, which, by the way, is less than market price to-day. We do not know of any dealer who is offering seeds at a penny apiece. If you will take the trouble to figure this up, you will find that, if a bed could be grown to average one hundred seeds to each plant, the seed crop would be worth $1089 to the square rod, or $174,240 per acre.

"On the other hand—on a different soil—the writer had a bed of five hundred plants in which, owing to the wet weather in the early part of the season, every one of the plants died down during the month of June. We expect a few of them will come up this season. There is no question but that the ginseng business offers a big chance for making money—and also a big chance for losing money, if not well handled."

It is probable that at this time, if not before, the would-be grower will ask if the prices demanded for plants and seeds are reasonable, and if the possible profits to be derived in the business warrant the outlay of his money. Since the author believes that there is now no one sending turnip and similar seed, nor wild sarsaparilla plants, instead of ginseng seed and plants, he will confine his remarks to ginseng prices and leave this type of fraud without further comment. It is his candid opinion that the prices some men demand are far too high, and the exactions that others impose as to the number of plants or seeds they will sell to one person are ridiculous. With respect to other dealers, the whole matter rests upon the law of supply and demand. Ginseng growing is on the boom and investors must expect to pay high prices.

Knowing that first-class fruit trees can be purchased for twenty cents, and acknowledging a weakness for fruit, the author would hesitate to pay the sum mentioned for a little plant smaller than an undersized, unmarketable radish that he can't eat, and five cents for a single seed, knowing also that if he should succeed in making the things grow, he must wait four or five years before he can sell the root. No, he has not forgotten that the plant will produce seed (it simply can't help doing that!) and that this seed will be worth so much at present prices, nor that it may be planted, and that, and that, and that! He has not forgotten this, but he knows that it is mostly on paper. What if the plant should die? It possibly will if the grower has had no experience. What if the price should fall? No. While the author has no fault to find with the man who asks high prices, he nevertheless thinks that after the boom, sellers of ginseng nursery stock will be glad to get $5 a hundred for one-year-old roots, and $1 an ounce for seed of even named varieties, and that at these prices they should make money. Until that time arrive, however, the man who wants to grow ginseng must expect to pay for his fun. If he could only put himself in the seller's place how quickly prices would fall!

But, joking aside, the only conclusion to be drawn from the conditions presented in the preceding and the present sections, are that prices of both roots and seeds must decline, that the prices of dried root must also fall, that fraud will be exposed and that the industry, now afflicted with the rickets and only commencing to toddle, will outgrow its weakness and finally stand firmly. These conclusions are also in harmony with what the consuls in China and Korea have to say of the ginseng industry in general. A careful perusal of the letters that follow should give the would-be grower hope that even should he pay exorbitant prices for stock he can look forward to profitable returns. No further comment need be made than to say that these quotations are either entire letters or the important parts of such as have appeared since the first edition of this book was published. They are arranged, as will be seen, according to the dates upon which they were written.

THE ASIATIC GINSENG INDUSTRY AND MARKET

Consul-General Rounsevelle Wildman, writing from Hong Kong, January 7, 1898, says in United States Consular Reports, Vol. 56 (1898):

"The price of ginseng, like the price of deerhorn, is governed more by sentiment than by the law of supply and demand. It depends upon the color, the form and size, and its fancied resemblance to the human body. Two pieces of ginseng, both weighing the same and both of the same color and taken from the ground at the same time, might vary one hundred per cent in price; and yet there is no real reason, to occidental eyes, for the distinction. The preferred variety is thin, and has two lateral arms projecting from the stem.

"Of course no such price as $100 an ounce is ever under any circumstances paid for the American growth, although I have seen mandarin ginseng that was worth one hundred and thirty-five times its own weight in silver. As a general statement, American ginseng will sell here for $3 to $3.50 (gold) per pound. It would not sell for less, and might, if properly exploited, bring ten times that much. I mean, if it were exhibited in such a way that the Chinese could buy it, piece by piece, as fish or chickens are bought, in the public market, instead of by the quantity.

"All the leading Chinese merchants come to this consulate weekly, and samples of American ginseng could be sent in care of the consulate, spread on a table, and the Chinese merchants could send orders to America with the samples. The market for a good article is practically unlimited. There are 400,000,000 Chinese, and all to some extent use ginseng. If they can once become satisfied with the results obtained from the tea made of the American ginseng, the yearly demand will run up into the millions of dollars' worth. The mandarin or imperial ginseng ($50 to $200 an ounce) is beyond the reach of the majority, and the Korean ginseng is used more as a tonic than as a panacea. Hong Kong is a free port, so the only expense of sending ginseng would be freight across the continent and across the Pacific to Hong Kong.

"As to packing, that is a question to be decided on the quality and condition of the article. Of course, the crude root would come in tight boxes or barrels, but the clarified would demand more care. If the exporter wished to test the market in competition with the Manchurian ginseng, I would advise him to pack in cotton, so there could be no possible breakage, or even rubbing of one root against another. In any case, the clarified root—rendered translucent by steaming, skimming, and drying—should be packed carefully, so as not to break.

"The little part or nub, where the arms join the stem, is considered of far greater value than the lower section, while the part above ground is not eaten at all; it is supposed to be injurious. Consequently, if the nub is broken off, two-thirds of the value of the root would be gone. It must be attached to the body. Good ginseng breaks easily."

Only a few days later (January 24, 1898) Minister Horace N. Allen wrote from Seoul, Korea, as follows:

"Korea is noted for the superior excellence of its ginseng, which brings a higher price in China than that imported from other countries. Although the Koreans, the Chinese, and, to a certain extent, the Japanese, are greatly addicted to the use of this drug, the Chinese, by virtue of their vast numbers, are the chief purchasers of the root. The import of American ginseng into China for the year 1896, according to Chinese customs returns, was 264,860 catties, valued at

1,033,882 taels (equal to 353,147 pounds, valued at $656,515 gold), or about $1.86 gold per pound.

"Korean ginseng declared at the same ports for the year 1896 amounted to 11,240 catties, valued at 389,192 taels (14,987 pounds, valued at $247,137 gold), or about $16.50 per pound. It may be seen that by customs valuations alone, the Korean ginseng is appraised at nearly nine times the value of that from America.

"The above declared amount of ginseng imported into China from Korea is supposed to represent not more than half of the actual importation, as the smuggling of this article is made the business of almost every Chinaman returning home from Korea. There is also a considerable import of Korean ginseng into Hong Kong, which being a British port, is not included in the reports of the Chinese customs.

"The Korean ginseng crop for 1896, marketed early in 1897 and declared at the customs, amounted in round numbers to 31,000 catties (41,300 pounds); valued in Korea at 600,000 yen ($300,000 gold), on which an export duty of 300,000 yen ($150,000 gold) was collected. The value of this crop in China is considerably more than double its valuation in Korea, the best Korean ginseng often bringing 50 taels ($31.75 gold per pound) in China.

"Numerous requests are received at this office from time to time for ginseng seeds. It will be seen from reading this report that it is useless to send the seeds to America, as they will dry out on the way and fail to germinate when planted."

"American Ginseng in China" is the title of an article in Consular Reports prepared by Consul-General Rounsevelle Wildman on January 7, 1900, which is quoted entire as follows:

"The demand for a market for American ginseng in China continues. I am in receipt by every mail of letters from all parts of the United States asking for market quotations of ginseng and for the names of buyers here. In my previous report on ginseng, dated January 7, 1898, I said in brief that it would be absolutely necessary for buyers here to see the stuff before purchasing, as the purchaser will not take the word of another as to quality or condition; that Chinese buy their ginseng after carefully sorting it themselves, and would no more think of purchasing at a distance than we would buy a horse with our eyes blindfolded. I further suggested that if American exporters cared to send a shipment of ginseng to my care, I would personally see that it was submitted to the Chinese buyers, and obtain an opinion from them as to the possibility of finding a profitable market on this coast. One American dealer in ginseng (a resident of Pennsylvania) alone took advantage of my offer. On July 8, 1899, he shipped to my care a box of American ginseng containing eighteen and one-half pounds, of which he says:

" 'I saved some of my last year's crop especially to send you. I am sending three grades. The market in New York last year went ninety cents higher than ever before, and has opened this year $1.75 higher than ever before. I think that the price will reach $7 per pound. . . . The question comes up many times in this country as to what use is made of our ginseng in China, and I should like very much to be informed.'

"The last question was answered in my previous report.

"The sample box of ginseng arrived, and it was found that no care had been taken in the packing, and no attention was paid to the directions clearly laid down in my previous report. The three grades were more or less mixed and broken, and, worse still, were somewhat damp. All this could have been easily guarded against by careful packing. As the sender was in no hurry for its sale, I concluded to hold it, to note the effect of the dry season upon it, and also to give different Chinese buyers a chance to look it over thoroughly. The lot proved far too small in bulk and too mixed in grades to dispose of as a whole or to thoroughly test the fluctuating market. The box contained a few excellent pieces, some medium, much small, some strings, and a fair proportion of broken pieces known as dust. The lot therefore required picking over and sorting into grades before the Chinese would bid for it. Even the largest shipments of ginseng are sold only after thorough inspection and sorting. This is one of the rules of the trade, to which there seems to be no exception. This practice, I may add, has become general, in consequence, the Chinese say, of the failure of American and Japanese exporters to maintain the standard of their shipments. They declare that their second and subsequent shipments are never equal to their first; so that any ginseng that might be shipped would have to be sorted. There is a very large business done here in ginseng, all of which is in the hands of the Chinese. This being a free port and without a custom house, no reliable record is obtainable of the quantity imported, and the Chinese never keep statistics. There is an endless variety of ginseng used, but for convenience it may be broadly classified as follows:

"*Yung Sum*—First quality from or near Pekin.

"*Korea Yung Sum*—Second quality from Korea.

"*Far Kee Yung Sum*—Third quality from America.

"It is estimated that last year about 3000 piculs (400,000 pounds) of the first quality was imported, about 500 to 600 piculs (66,666 to 80,000 pounds) of the second, and some 3000 piculs of the third. The Pekin ginseng is pinkish in appearance, very hard and smooth, and is free from roots and small pieces The second is rather opaque and otherwise resembles the first.

"My correspondent's lot embraces values all the way from $12 to $40 Mexican per catty (one catty equals one and one-third pounds), while the dust will not bring over $2 Mexican a pound. These prices are quite satisfactory, considering his statement regarding New York quotations. There is no reason why there should not be a large and growing market for American ginseng, and I would like to see it thoroughly exploited. This can be done only by sending a trial shipment of, say, two thousand pounds of selected pieces, the large pieces, of course, being the best.

"Instead of shipping to this consulate in the future, I would recommend that all merchants correspond direct with Mr. A. O'D. Gourdin, of Hong Kong, who is personally known to me and who would give the matter his careful attention. There are no Chinese firms here with whom it would be possible for the American exporter to deal direct. The American ginseng that comes to this market is for the most part purchased by Chinese firms located in New York and shipped hither at a great profit to themselves, so that it would be very much to the advantage of the American exporter to deal direct with a responsible agent here. I trust that this report will be read in connection with my previous one, for I believe that if the exporter will follow out the directions contained in both, there will be little difficulty in disposing on this coast of all the ginseng that is grown in America."

On January 28, 1902, Consul-General W. A. Rublee writes an article with the same title in United States Consular Reports, Vol. 69, which article is also quoted in full:

"The sale of ginseng root grown in America, about which there have been several inquiries at this consulate by interested parties in the United States, is very considerable in Hong Kong, and the demand is so great that much more could be disposed of advantageously. The ginseng root is as indispensable to the well-to-do Chinese as is their rice. They attribute all sorts of medicinal virtues to the root, especially using it as a stimulant. The growth of the ginseng trade has been marked in recent years, and higher prices are now paid by dealers than ever before, especially during the last three years. American growers of ginseng may confidently expect a steadily increasing market in Hong Kong, although it is largely only a distributing center. The root is prepared in this city. The skin is cleaned and smoothed by a special process, sorted out in equal sizes, put up in neat boxes of various capacities, according to quality, and re-exported to all the consuming districts in China. The bulk of the shipments goes to the northern ports, such as Shanghai, Hankan, Tientsin, and Chefoo, although a fair proportion finds its way to Canton and the coast ports— Amoy, Swatow, and Fuchau; also to Formosa, and other markets where there are Chinese.

"The average value of American ginseng annually received at Hong Kong is from $1,700,000 to $1,800,000 Mexican ($763,300 to $808,200 gold). On January 1, 1902, the Mexican dollar was valued by the United States Mint at forty-four and nine-tenths cents.

"The value of the Chinese ginseng annually imported is estimated at about $100,000 Mexican ($44,900). The quantity is small, but its value is computed at twenty to forty times its weight in silver, according to quality. The importation of Korean ginseng root is valued at about $800,000 ($359,200) a year.

"The prices of ginseng vary according to quality. The wild, dried American root, as imported at Hong Kong, may be classified into three grades, generally known to the trade as 'fair,' 'good,' and 'extra' or 'selected.' The values per picul (one hundred thirty-three and one-third pounds) of these grades, as based on sales made during the last three years, were:

GRADE	VALUE	
	Mexican	Gold
Fair	$1420	$637.58
Good	1560	700.34
Selected	1930	866.57

"The present values of these grades bring the price in American currency, respectively, per pound, to $4.05, $5.25, and $6.18, after deducting charges, trade discount, selling and guarantee commissions. This latter estimate is furnished by an experienced and reliable local dealer.

"In addition to the grades mentioned above, others are imported, and among the best is some picked root worth $4460 to $4500 Mexican ($2002.54 to $2020.50) per picul (one hundred thirty-three and one-third pounds). Split root (cut lengthwise in two pieces) may be quoted at $1500 Mexican ($673.50) per picul. Siftings (chips and dust) are also salable at $120 to $130 Mexican ($53.88 to $58.37) per picul. Very little cultivated American root has so far been imported into Hong Kong. The value of a few small shipments averaged $3200 Mexican ($1426.80) per picul. The cultivated root was much liked by the native buyers, and its cultivation ought to be encouraged in the United States.

"The Korean ginseng root brings higher prices than that from the United States Korean root in the Hong Kong market is quoted as follows, per picul (one hundred thirty-three and one-third pounds):

| DESCRIPTION | VALUE ||
	Mexican	Gold
20 roots to the pound	$6500	$2918.50
30 roots to the pound	5500	2469.50
40 roots to the pound	4500	2020.50

"American ginseng growers should be careful to conform to the requirements of the Chinese markets. The principal points are cleanliness, good color (bright yellow), and freedom from dust and chips. It is desirable that the root be sorted before it is shipped, so that the better qualities may be sold separately. However, even unassorted ginseng root of any quality is salable according to its merit. Ginseng may be shipped in any quantity, and should be packed in strong wooden casks or cases of a capacity of from one hundred to two hundred pounds. Old whiskey casks might be used, but they should be quite dry before the root is packed. If the root is packed in a wet condition, it becomes moldy and deteriorates. The clarified root is liked by purchasers here, and its value is, as a rule, higher than that of the crude root. There is no particular process of clarification in Hong Kong, but the Korean root is clarified with honey.

"American ginseng exporters desirous of making shipments to Hong Kong will find it to their advantage to communicate with F. J. V. Jorge, 24 Bank Buildings, Hong Kong. Mr. Jorge has handled American ginseng for over twenty years and is perhaps the most experienced Hong Kong merchant in this line. He has recently established an independent commission business, and is in a position to act as agent for American firms. I mention his name in order that those interested in the ginseng trade may, if they so desire, enter into business relations with someone in Hong Kong. Mr. Jorge can doubtless furnish satisfactory references through the banks, and his familiarity with the ginseng trade recommends him to American exporters of this article."

Mr. S. Iida writes of the condition of "Ginseng in Korea" as follows in *American Gardening*, March 1, 1902:

"There seems to be a renewal of the once perennial trouble about ginseng in Korea. This valuable root is grown in considerable quantities in the peninsula, especially in the neighborhood of Kaisong, in Kyong-ki-do, which is near Seoul. The cultivators have never been allowed to dispose of the root on their own account. The business has always been a government monopoly. In old times, when Korea sent annual tribute to China, her envoys used to carry with them the year's exportable supply of ginseng, which they sold as best they could to Chinese merchants. But when Korea acquired her independence, under Japan's auspices, in 1896, it became necessary for the Seoul authorities to provide some other means of disposing of the root. They therefore established agencies at suitable places in China.

"Meanwhile, Japanese adventurers, taking advantage of the discontent caused among the cultivators by the extremely low prices at which they were compelled to part with their produce to the government, repaired to Kaisong, and succeeded in obtaining large quantities of the root. Things went merrily enough until this illegal trading began to bear its inevitable fruit. Some of the Japanese, secure against open complaint on the part of the Korean cultivators, obtained supplies of ginseng on the credit of promissory notes which they never redeemed.

"Finally these irregularities became so flagrant that, after much consultation, it was decided to entrust to a Japanese firm the whole business of selling the ginseng. The Mitsui Bussan Kaisha were selected, and since last year they have been carrying on the work, paying cash to the government immediately on receipt of the root and then exporting and disposing of it at the firm's risk. It is a big business, involving a floating capital of over a million yen annually, and whether the results have thus far been favorable to the Japanese firm we do not know, but rumor says that they do not succeed in collecting their money from the Chinese consumers as promptly as they themselves pay over the purchase price to the Korean authorities. The point is, however, that a new invasion of adventurers has taken place at Kaisong, this being the time for harvesting the crop, and that some seventy persons, Japanese and Koreans in collusion, are resorting to all sorts of devices to evade the official monopoly. Application has been made by the Korean government to Mr. Hayashi, and it is said that the matter is causing some trouble."

Minister H. N. Allen, of Seoul, under date of May 28, 1902, sends a report on the Korean ginseng crop for 1901, as follows:

"The crop of Korean ginseng for 1901 has been sold to a Japanese firm for 1,255,500 yen ($625,239). It amounted, with beard, to 52,000 catties (68,120 pounds). After purchasing this ginseng, the purchasers deliberately burned 10,000 catties (13,100 pounds), as the supply was in excess of the demand. It is said that a considerable portion of last year's supply still remains unsold in China, and that this year's crop in Korea was enough for nearly three years' consumption. The market is limited, as the Chinese are about the only consumers. Although ginseng is regularly raised in various parts of Korea, only that raised upon the imperial farms at Songdo is said to have the real virtues claimed for the root as a medicine. These Songdo plantations are the only ones that are guarded with care. The soil is a disintegrated granite. For the past few years the annual crop has been growing larger; 15,000 catties (19,650 pounds) has been regarded as the normal quantity, but by gathering it at five years instead of seven, and by increasing the number of beds, the supply has finally exceeded the demand. This must be of interest to the number of Americans who have of late gone into ginseng culture."

In reply to inquiries by a New York correspondent, Consul James W. Ragsdale, of Tientsin, under date of June 26, 1902, writes in Consular Reports:

"There are four principal kinds of ginseng known to the trade—the native, which comes from Kirin and its neighborhood; the Korean, the American, and the Japanese. Miraculous healing properties are ascribed to the Kirin ginseng, and it commands a very high price, the best specimens being sold at two hundred to six hundred times their weight in silver. Only the wealthy, of course, can indulge in this costly drug, but such is the faith of all classes of China in the life-giving virtues of the plant that even the poorer classes make tremendous sacrifices to obtain it, in cases of emergency. Owing to the immense demand and the limited supply in the wild state, the farmers near Kirin are doing a thriving business in cultivating ginseng, although it commands only a fraction of the price that is paid for it in a wild condition.

"Korean ginseng is next in cost, the prices ranging from $5 to $75 ($2.07 to $31.12) per catty (one and one-third pounds), according to size and quality, one Mexican dollar equaling forty-one and one-half cents The consumption of Korean ginseng must be enormous, but no statistics are available, as most of it is smuggled over the border from Korea to China.

"American ginseng is becoming more widely known and more popular every year, especially in the southern provinces. In the last few years, the prices paid for it have more than doubled. In the province of Chinkiang, American ginseng is in special demand. Almost everybody takes it in the spring as a tonic. The retail prices prevailing at present are:

DESCRIPTION	PRICE	
	Mexican	United States
Best, per ounce	$2.50	$1.04
Good to fair, do	1.00	.415
Fair to common, do	$0.50 to 1.00	$0.207 to .415

"The cheapest ginseng comes from Japan; it is used principally by those who cannot afford the other kinds.

"There can be no doubt that a profitable business can be done in this article, if the trade is properly pushed by Chinese agents of good social standing. Wild ginseng [Manchurian] commands a much higher price in China than the cultivated article."

LETTERS FROM GROWERS

An attempt was made to get letters of experiences from many growers throughout the land for the purpose of including them in this book. It is to be regretted, however, that so few men were willing to write at all and that the majority of those who did send letters, wrote so little that might be of interest to the general reader. Since the author wishes to keep in close touch with ginseng culture as it gradually but surely rises to the dignity of an industry, he will keep a register of growers and dealers. He, therefore, requests all such to send him their addresses on a postal card, with the words ginseng grower, or ginseng dealer, etc.

Mr. George C. Foulk describes in Foreign Relations of the United States, 1885, the ginseng gardens of Korea and the methods of growing the crop there as follows:

"Each farm is a rectangular compound, one part containing the buildings inclosed by walls, the rest by hedges. The buildings, though built as usual of mud, stones, earthenware, and untrimmed timbers, and thatched, are strikingly superior to the other houses of the Korean people. They are built in right lines, interiors neatly arranged, and walks and hedges in good order. In each compound are one or more tall little watch towers, in which a regular lookout is held over the farm to prevent raids of thieves, who might make off with paying amounts in handfuls of ginseng.

"Beyond the buildings, occupying the remaining space in the compound, are parallel rows of low, dark mat sheds, with roofs sloping downward toward the south or southwest. These rows are from seventy-five to two hundred feet long and four feet apart, and the mat sheds about four feet high at their front (north) sides, which are closed by mats which swing from the top, thus giving access to the farmer in his care of the plants. Within the sheds are beds about eight inches high for the growing ginseng plants, which are in rows extending across the beds, about two feet long.

"The row (or shed) nearest the houses is the seed bed for all the plants grown on the farm. . . . In the Korean ninth month (September-October) the seeds are stuck quite thickly in the seed bed to a depth of three inches in little watering trenches about three inches apart. Once in each three days' interval during its whole life the plant is watered, and the bed carefully inspected to prevent crowding, decay, and the ravages of worms and insects. The mat shed is kept closely shut, for ginseng will only grow in the dark or a very weak light.

"The mats of the sheds are made of round, brown reeds and vines closely stitched together, admitting only the faintest light.

"In the second month of the second year after

108   PRESENT STATUS OF THE INDUSTRY.

planting (February) the root is regarded as formed

FIG 18. KOREAN GINSENG

and the general shape of the plant above ground

attained. [A typical Korean ginseng root, engraved from a photograph, furnished by Mr. H. P. Kelsey, is shown in Fig. 18.] The shape is nearly that of the matured plant. . . . In the following February (of the third year) the seed plants are transplanted to the adjoining beds, five or six to each cross row, the watering trenches being here between the plant rows. In this second bed the plants remain one year, and are then transplanted to the third bed, and planted still farther apart in their respective rows. A year later they are again transplanted, this time to their final beds, where they remain two and a half or three years. Generally speaking, seven years are required from the time of planting until the plant is matured. After its life in the seed bed, exacting care in keeping out the light is not so necessary, and I noticed the swinging mat was removed entirely from the fronts of sheds of plants in the final beds."

Mr. Nicholas Pike, formerly United States Consul at Port Louis, Mauritius, writes of the Chinese methods thus:

"Two methods of cultivating ginseng are followed by the Chinese, viz., growing from seed, and transplanting young plants found in the wild state. A spot is selected in the dark, damp woods, generally where the soil is rich and loamy. The seeds are gathered when they drop from the plant to the ground. After the soil is dug over, these seeds are sown broadcast, and covered with dead leaves partially decomposed. This plantation they call their nursery. In from fifteen to eighteen months the young shoots appear above the ground, and as soon as they are two or three inches high they are removed to the permanent plantation, and in three years more the roots are ready for the market. Whenever a root is taken from the ground a young plant is set in its place, so that a plantation once formed is producing all the time."

Messrs. E. D. and M. S. Crosley, Tula, N. Y.: "As to the expense of seed and plants, we paid during the years 1897, 1899 and 1900, $44.50. The plants that we bought were wild roots purchased at from eighty cents to $1 a pound. We have set only thrifty plants and have dried and sold enough to pay more than the whole cost. We dug what we could ourselves. So our only expense for enough to set one-half acre at Tula and 28,000 in Truxton was $44.50.

"By carefully studying the analyses of the root, and by experimenting to find the best way to apply fertilizers from the start, we have found that it is possible to produce eight-ounce roots in four years from small wild roots. Cultivated roots grow more evenly and produce a greater average of seed."

Mr. B. L. Hart, Rose Hill, N. Y.: "We dug a small portion of one of our beds of four-year-old roots in October to note the weights of the roots, and the largest of them weighed five ounces, green, while the smallest weighed three ounces, making an average of about four ounces to the root, green. Three pounds of the cultivated roots, green, will make one pound of the dry.

"We raised in the neighborhood of 300,000 seedlings the past season and judged that ninety per cent of the seeds we sowed in the fall of 1900 germinated and produced plants. In this section the seed crop was rather light, on account of so much unfavorable wet weather, but our three-year-old plants made a yield of about sixty seeds to the plant.

"It is very true that there has been but a limited amount of figures given of the yield and profits in cultivating ginseng from actual shipments, and from what we can see at present, it will be several years before the enterprise will develop to this extent. Our present gardens cover an area of one and one-quarter acres, which is stocked with in the neighborhood of

250,000 and 300,000 plants of different ages. The oldest will be five in the spring and we have also planted a large amount of seeds of the 1900 crop that will produce plants this spring."

Mr. Charles B. Parent, Birchton, N Y.: "In the fall of 1896 I began the cultivation of ginseng by planting about a thousand roots; the next fall two hundred more roots and two ounces of seed; in 1898, two hundred roots and five ounces of seed; in 1899, three hundred roots and twelve ounces of seed. In 1900 I transplanted from my nursery bed three hundred and fifty roots and sowed about one pound of seed. Previous to 1900 I bought my increase of roots. In 1901 I transplanted about twenty-nine hundred roots and planted about a pound of seeds.

"In the fall, 1901, I dug from my oldest bed of roots to the amount of eight and one-half pounds, dried. Seven and one-half pounds sold for $7.50 per pound—the product of about fifteen square feet of ground. Previous to this digging I had taken out three pounds nine ounces, dried. These were removed for the purpose of thinning out, the plants being somewhat crowded. I have now an area of one hundred feet by forty-eight stocked with roots and seeds, the roots from one to six years old and seed that will come up next spring, 1902. The dried roots sold yielded $198.74. Since beginning I value the seeds at $500—not a high valuation. [A partial view of Mr. Parent's ginseng garden at Ballston Spa, N. Y., is seen in Fig. 19.]

"Anyone thinking of growing this root for market should take into consideration the time required to place the business on a paying basis. If good two-year-old roots be planted they should become marketable in four years—six years from the seed. This is not an estimate of what should be, but what can be done if proper care be given the plant during this whole time of growth. Some will grow a good article of a certain vegetable or fruit while another will not; attention to details is essential in this line as in other works. The statement has been made that ginseng

FIG 10. CHARLES B. PARENT'S GINSENG GARDENS, BALLSTON SPA, N. Y.

"is easy to raise." I have found it required something besides ease to grow a good article. I have carried this work along in connection with other farm work."

Mr. C. D. Nusbaum, Jonesboro, Ill.: "In May, 1900, I selected a number of roots from a lot that had been washed clean and brought to market, and set them under the lattice in my nursery; they are now growing nicely. Transplanting in the spring, however, after the leaf stock has appeared will retard the growth for that season, consequently it is best to do transplanting either early in the spring, say during March and April, before the tops appear, or in the fall after the plant has attained its growth for the season. In this locality (southern Illinois) planting may be begun August 1st and continue till the ground freezes.

"The two principal requirements in ginseng culture are rich soil and shade. The kind of soil does not matter so much just so it is rich in humus or decayed vegetable matter. My nursery is situated on ordinary clay soil that is well-drained upland and was fertilized with well-rotted horse manure and woods soil. The location of a ginseng garden should always be on land that is well drained and level or sloping toward the north or east. A lattice shade should be erected on posts high enough to allow one to walk erect under it. The lattice may be made of ordinary plastering lath nailed on one-half inch apart. In the North where the snowfall is heavy the lattice should be made in sections eight feet long so that it can be removed in winter. [The arrangement of these lattice frames, together with some eight to ten-year-old wild plants transplanted from the forest in the fall of 1900, are shown in Fig. 20.]

"Under this lattice the beds should be made, leaving an eighteen-inch walk between each pair of beds; four feet is a convenient width for the beds and they should be framed with eight-inch boards held in place by stakes. It is necessary to have the walks between the beds so that the beds can be attended to without stepping on the soil. If one is starting in a small way and does not care to incur the expense of erecting the lattice on posts the beds may be framed twelve to fifteen inches high, making them four feet wide and

FIG 20. VIEW OF A CORNER IN ONE OF C. D. NUSBAUM'S GINSENG GARDENS

any length convenient. Then the lattice may be made in sections four feet square and placed on the frames; they may be removed when the beds need attention.

"To prepare the beds spread on a good dressing of horse manure and work deeply, making the soil loose and porous by mixing the manure well with it. Give the beds a dressing of rich humus three or four inches deep and mix this well with the soil. This will put old and poor ground in good condition for ginseng. If the ground be rich garden soil so much the better, but treat it in the same way. If humus or rich woods soil cannot be obtained work in plenty of manure and unleached wood ashes. After mixing well and pulverizing, level off the beds smoothly and they will be ready to plant.

"The roots should be set six or seven inches apart each way, which will give them ample room to grow to a marketable size. A good device for setting roots is a planting board. Take two boards six or seven inches wide and long enough to fit down easily crosswise in the beds and nail light strips across at the ends and center to hold them together to keep them from warping. Cut notches seven inches apart on one edge and place this edge of the board where you want to begin planting. Now with a spade open a trench deep enough to accommodate the longest roots, place the roots at the notches, being careful to plant them deep enough so that the bud at the top of the roots will be one and one-half to two inches under the soil when covered, and draw the soil to them, pressing it firmly around the roots, then level off. Now place the board seven inches further on for the next row and so continue. Do not step on the beds where roots have been planted but stand on the planting board while at work. When done planting give the beds a light dressing of manure or humus and cover with a mulch of dry leaves three or four inches deep and lay on some brush to keep the leaves from blowing off. Be sure to remove the brush in the spring but let the leaf mulch remain.

"No stirring of the ground or cultivation will be necessary except to keep the beds free from grass and weeds; this should be done with the hand, as the roots might be injured by using a hoe or other tool. Each fall after the tops have died down, give the beds a light dressing of humus, pulverized well-rotted manure or unleached wood ashes, and a mulching of leaves for protection during the winter and to conserve moisture during the hot months of summer. Some wood ashes sprinkled on the beds while the plants are growing makes a good fertilizer; just apply the ashes without removing the mulch.

"The seeds begin to ripen early in August and should be gathered as they ripen, and as it takes them eighteen months as a rule to germinate they should be stratified in sifted soil in a strong box, which may be kept in a cellar and kept moist by watering occasionally, as the seed should not be allowed to dry out thoroughly. [Don't keep too wet, because the seeds may rot.] The box may be buried outside, letting it in the ground till the top is three or four inches below the surface. The seed should be kept in this manner for twelve months, or until the following fall, and then planted.

"After the roots have reached a good marketable size, which, if two-year-old roots have been planted will be in from three to four years, they should be dug carefully, so as not to cut or bruise them, and washed clean. They may then be dried in the sun or in a moderate artificial heat, care being taken to prevent burning or scorching them. They will then be ready to pack in clean boxes for market."

Mr. John Fraser, Salem, N. Y.: "Select any good corn land; better take that which is free of stone, or remove all stone to the depth of one foot. If the ground be in sod, manure it well and crop the first year with corn, cabbage, or some other farm crop. In selecting a location better keep away from shade trees and all woodland. All experienced growers agree that the best results are obtained by garden or field culture, under shade.

"Having the ground free of stone and other obstructions, use well-rotted manure at the rate of one farm load to two square rods of ground. See that the manure is well rotted, fine and well broken up. Ginseng is not a foliage plant but a root plant; therefore avoid all fresh manure. Mix the manure with the soil as evenly as possible and divide the ground into beds about five feet wide. The beds should be made by driving stakes in the ground, nailing five-inch boards to the stakes, and leaving a walk sixteen inches wide between the beds.

"For sowing seed, sift fine manure through a three-fourths inch mesh sieve and cover the bed one inch deep. Then mix this manure with the surface soil of the bed. I prefer to do it with the sieve. Now, level the bed smoothly and mark with a four-inch marker; in these marks press a clapboard, beveled to an edge, one inch deep. Sow in these cracks either seed or berries about one inch apart and after sowing go over each row with the sharp edge of the board and gently press each seed or berry to the bottom of the crack. Cover the seed by drawing the board angling across the rows; then cover the beds with leaves three or four inches deep. Some lay brush on to keep the leaves in place, but I have never been bothered by the wind.

"When the plantlets are coming up remove the leaves and sow on the bed hardwood ashes at the rate of one peck per square rod; and again in two or three weeks when all plants have appeared repeat the application. The potash destroys and drives away numerous insects that feed on the young plants and prevents slumping off. Do not use any nitrate of soda or other fertilizers rich in nitrogen; such are injurious to the plants.

"For setting roots we mark the beds both ways with a six-inch marker, using a dibber to make the hole in each square and inserting the root with the crown two inches below the surface. With the forefinger hold the root in place, again insert the dibber an inch from the hole, pressing the earth firmly against the root, especially at the lower end, and smooth off with the hand. For setting southern roots use a dibber three inches wide to make room for the numerous fibers or rootlets. Northern roots are straight like a young parsnip with very few rootlets. A dibber that will answer very well may be made by cutting about fourteen inches from the top of a fork handle and sharpening to a point.

"After setting cover the beds with fine rotten manure about an inch deep, and leaves or swale grass three or four inches deep, which latter must be removed in the spring. We prepare our beds in the fall for setting roots in the spring—we dig and set all our cultivated roots in April. Then we need no leaf mulching and we find that roots set in the spring will not miss one in a hundred. They will come up better and bear more seed than those set in the fall, but people who buy roots or who dig wild roots cannot set in the spring, as the time for spring setting is limited on account of the quickness of the plant developing its bud.

"Several years ago my son and I thought we would try growing ginseng. We had no experience but had read up everything we could find that had been printed on the subject. To make a careful start we bought in the fall three hundred two-year-old roots and three ounces of stratified seed that would come up the next May. We selected three kinds of soil—clay loam, sandy loam, and slate loam in three different fields on the farm—made a seed bed in each field, three and a half feet wide by twelve feet long, by standing boards four inches wide on their edges around each bed. We sowed one ounce of seed and set one hundred roots in each bed, covered with leaves for the winter, fenced in each bed with a board fence, and in the spring shaded the beds with lath and brush. The bed that had the

FIG 21. SETTING GINSENG PLANTS AT THE BATES GINSENG GARDENS, CUBA, N. Y.

brush was just as good as the lath covered bed but not

so tidy or convenient. About every root grew and about eighty-five seeds out of a hundred came up and did well all summer. We were so favorably impressed with the way all three pieces prospered that we bought several thousand roots and four pounds of seed the next fall and enlarged our grounds so that to-day we can say we are in the swim. The three hundred two-year-old roots weighed at the time of planting four and one-half pounds. At the end of the third season, when five years old, we dug forty-five pounds of green roots. Besides, we had three years' seed, and the last year's seed crop was worth twice as much as the cost of the roots and expenses of the three years' cultivation.

"Some say: 'I would like to grow ginseng but it takes too long; I cannot wait six or eight years for returns.' We are glad that Nature has so fixed it that man cannot shorten the time, for there is where the great money profit comes in. Some advertise not over twenty-five roots at thirty cents per root and not over one hundred seeds at two cents each to one person; another advertises to have ginseng growing in the far South, or on the mountain tops. We think it best to fling a little shy of these gentlemen, because our best growers, who never advertise, and yet have more than they can do to take care of the present demand for the roots, make no such statements.

"We have seen a number start to grow ginseng by getting a few roots and seeds and planting them in fence corners partly protected by some sticks and boards. Soon after, these patches fail because some domestic animal destroys the whole thing. Our advice to those who wish to try ginseng culture is to read the matter up. Within the last three years there have been some good methods of its culture printed. Then go to some responsible grower and if he cannot supply roots and seeds at the market price he will in all probability know of someone who can. Put only a little money in at first. Try a bed four feet wide, ten feet long, with a good fence around it, and proper shade. Stock it with seed and roots With proper care its increase in a few years will be surprising."

Mr. W. A. Bates, Cuba, N. Y., has over an acre of ginseng under cultivation, scenes of which are presented herewith. Fig. 21 shows the process of setting the plants, and Fig. 22 presents a partial view of a shaded plantation.

Mr. Bernad A. Payson, Fingal, Ont., Canada: "The following is my experience in the ginseng business: About three years ago, I sent to Orange Judd Company and procured the book written by M. G. Kains on Ginseng Culture which I saw advertised in *Farm and Home*. I then started out to try and find if ginseng grew in our locality. The first afternoon, I found the plant thinly scattered through the woods on soil that did not dry out in summer nor become flooded in the wet season. I generally found the plant on a heavy sand or a black loam. The next three autumns I gathered wild roots in the woods during my spare time, and as is mentioned in the book, I cut off the roots which were attached to the necks of the plants and set them in the ground to grow buds, which some of them did. But I found that quite a lot of them would not produce buds although I left them in the ground for two years, so I have discontinued the practice. Another reason for stopping is that I think that a plant will produce more seed if the roots be not cut up but planted just as they are found.

"I have also found that wild roots dug in the woods and carefully planted in the clearing under cover, will start and grow very fast, in fact, I believe they will grow as much in one year in the garden as they would in three years in the woods. Wild plants, as a general rule, do not produce as much seed in the woods on

122 PRESENT STATUS OF THE INDUSTRY.

FIG 22. INTERIOR VIEW OF THE BATES GINSENG GARDENS, CUBA, N. Y.

account of too much shade. A plant that will produce from five to twenty seeds in the woods will, I believe, produce from twenty-five to one hundred and fifty in the clearing.

"In the stratifying of seeds, I have found that two-thirds leaf mold and one-third sand or loam, is a good mixture. I have had success with my seed put away in that preparation. I think that it is a good idea to have the seed box set out of doors under a lattice roof in the ginseng bed the following spring after the seed is gathered. It should be kept watered. Some of the seed will grow that spring and probably, by selection, a variety may be obtained, the seed of which will sprout the spring after it is gathered. I am working along this line. Since some seeds will start to grow while still stratified it is best to have depth enough at the bottom of the box below the seed for the roots to grow straight down, and not too much on the top, or it will be too deep for the young plants to get through.

"I have found that wild Canadian root, cultivated in the garden, will come up earlier in the spring, and ripen its seeds and its roots about three weeks earlier than the New York cultivated ginseng, thus giving the grower a better chance to dig and dry his crop of roots before the cold damp weather sets in, especially if it is to be dried in the heat of the sun.

"In regard to the distance between plants, I think that six inches each way is too close, especially for large plants. They will grow more seed, I believe, if not planted too closely. As to the proper time to plant seed, I think it does not make any very great difference as long as planting is done in the fall. I have planted seed when I had to shovel the snow off the ground, and at night had to cover the beds with boards to keep them from freezing. In regard to covering, I have found that brush has to be put on very thickly to take the place of lath, and I think that during a heavy fall of snow the roof might be crushed in.

"Concerning the preparation of the soil, too much work cannot be put on it in the way of enriching it [look out for too much nitrogen] and adding such things as will tend to keep the soil loose and of the same texture as the top soil is in the woods. I have found that the ginseng develops its fibrous roots in the direction in which the most nutriment lies; the main roots will do the same. It is advisable to have the soil richer at the bottom than at the top so as to produce

FIG 23. CORNER IN HARLAN P. KELSEY'S GINSENG NURSERY

a good, straight tap root and less side roots. I have found that the plants will send their fibrous roots straight up if the soil be very rich and moist on the surface.

"It is a good idea to watch the beds to see that mice do not work underneath the covering in the seed beds during the winter. I think it might be a good idea to put woven wire around the seed beds to protect them from mice."

[To show the extensive range of ginseng cultivation in America we present in Fig. 23 a corner in the ginseng gardens of Harlan P. Kelsey, Kawana, N. C.]

Mr. George Stanton, Apulia, N. Y.: "The Chinese ginseng farm at Apulia Station, N. Y., has now about fifty square rods of ground stocked with roots and seed sown. The seed crop of the past season was fifty pounds, which can be sold for $5 to $6 an ounce or $70 to $80 a pound, and was the product of less than a quarter of an acre of seed-bearing plants. Ginseng culture is having a great boom. Demand for stock much greater than supply. We closed the season this year with orders for more than six thousand roots which we could not supply. We had shipped more than 17,300 roots and nearly forty pounds seed during the season.

"We are learning the importance of thorough drainage for ginseng culture. Our experience with clay hard-pan subsoil and imperfect drainage has been very unsatisfactory, resulting in loss of roots from rot. Such soil should be tile drained. But, if possible, deep loamy soil should always be used; if slightly sandy all the better.

"We are also forcibly impressed with the importance of humus in the soil. This leads us to the natural conclusion that it is not safe to put ginseng into ground from which a crop of matured roots has been taken for market. Practical experience has confirmed this conclusion. Ginseng does not supply humus to the soil, and the four or six years required to produce a crop will entirely exhaust the humus. This is a lesson we did not like to learn. After putting up framework for shading and constructing beds we had hoped to replace the crop indefinitely. But nature has certain requirements that man must recognize or meet with disappointment.

"Another forcible argument against succession of crops is that disease and insect pests are likely to get into the soil, and though perhaps the smallest, nematodes are by no means of the least importance. While we do not know much about these minute creatures, their work is plainly visible in the form of nodules from the size of a turnip seed to that of a marble on the fibrous rootlets. Enlargements are often formed on the body of the root and around the neck also. I have seen them as large as a hen's egg on the neck of a root. When opened they show a large number of minute red cells in which the nematodes breed, though the outer surface is smooth and white. The tendency is to impair the vitality and lessen the seed production of the plant. In time softening and degeneration of the affected parts takes place, and ultimately more or less decay of the root. We think they also work in what seems like red rust on the bodies of roots, where they form slight depressions; and in the fibrous rootlets of old roots, destroying the entire system of feeders, resulting in consumption of root. We are coming to the conclusion that it may not be possible to cultivate ginseng without nematodes. We find them scattered over a considerable area, and not only in garden culture, but also on wild roots and in forest nurseries. Professor Slingerland says they are found on clematis roots and that they are a great pest in the German sugar beet fields. We have seen them on sugar beets in this country. We would caution against planting infected stock. When the nodules are confined to the rootlets they may be picked off, but, with all the precautions that may be taken, very likely they will be found when roots are dug for market. We think it will be fatal to put ginseng seed into ground known to be infected with nematodes.

"It should be the aim of every grower to produce the best possible quality of root for market in order to build up and maintain a high reputation for cultivated ginseng. The demand of the Chinese market is for solid, heavy roots. A large, light root is not as desirable as a heavy, small one. To reach best results, growth should be rapid and continuous, with liberal fertilizing. Roots should be taken up when in best prime condition. To determine how long they should be left in the ground to attain best results is a problem not easy to solve. From the experience and observation of ten years we have come to the conclusion that four to six years is long enough to keep transplanted roots in the ground. Much may depend upon soil, climate and other conditions, but it is safe to assume that when a bed of plants commences to go back, and the seed crop is less than the year before, the plants should be dug. It should be borne in mind that age does not indicate quality. We often find wild roots showing over sixty years' growth not nearly as large nor as heavy as some not more than fifteen or twenty years old. Like old people, after a certain age they lose their vitality and vigor.

"With the intensive culture applied to this plant we are producing heavy seed crops at the expense of seed production. With high price of seed the tendency is to keep roots in the ground too long. The real value of ginseng culture is production of root for the Chinese market, which is willing to pay good prices for *quality*. Selling seed and roots for planting is only incidental; the extremely high prices are likely to do the business more harm than good. To obtain best results in root production in shortest possible time, we think the seed head should be pinched off as soon as plants come up in the spring, thus throwing growth all into the roots. This, of course would be heroic treatment with seed at from $50 to $100 a pound, but we think it will come into general practice in the near future. It is not at all likely that the present high prices of seed will maintain many years, and it is not best that they should. Neither is it likely to go as low again as in the pioneer days of this industry. When the price gets so low that it no longer pays for its production, then take off the seed heads and develop root growth. I have often said to people visiting my grounds that the seed crop was a silver mine, while at the bottom of the plant was a gold mine. Better develop the gold mine, as that is destined to be the only true standard of value.

"Here let us emphasize the value of starting with good stock. We consider northern stock much more desirable than southern; northern ginseng commands a much higher price in the market than the southern. In the South it has assumed a fixed type known as 'nubbin' and 'peanut' ginseng. Northern grown seed is much larger than southern—some southern growers claim thirteen thousand seeds to the pound, while best grade northern seed runs about eight thousand to the pound. It stands to reason, and our own experience and observation bear it out, that large seed will produce large, strong plants from the start, other conditions being favorable. We are not making this statement in the interest of any particular geographical or local section but in the general interest of the business.

"We have observed a peculiar freak of ginseng seed which we have never observed in any other kind of seed, and that is, two separate, distinct stems from one seed and only one root. It is not the result of 'stooling out' or after development; the indication is that some of the seeds have double germs. It **does** not follow that all such roots will continue to develop two stems in after years. We have found some that had a germ for only one stem the second season. It is quite common for old roots to develop two or more stems. We have known a single root to send up six perfect stems in one season.

"The ginseng plant is a very interesting study and is always developing some new traits. It responds liberally to good treatment, will stand drouth as well as ordinary crops, is not seriously injured by ordinary frost, but hard freezing is likely to kill some of the plants and seriously injure the seed crop. Do not sprinkle the plants when frosted as it would likely injure the seed crop; at least, such has been our experience and observation at the Chinese ginseng farm.

"Ginseng plants are liable to some kind of disease the cause and nature of which we have as yet been unable to determine. First indications are wilting and drooping of part or all of the plant, leaves turning black and drying, stalk shrinking and withering for a few inches from the top down to, and sometimes below the surface of the ground. In this case the stalk is generally soft and degenerated, the disease extending to the root, which sooner or later is likely to decay. We have not been able to determine whether the disease first commences in the root or the plant. We know that the plants sometimes prematurely die and leaves drop off while the root seems to be sound and healthy. If on pulling up an affected plant the stalk readily comes up with a portion of the neck showing disintegration, with strong offensive odor, it indicates root-rot. But if the stalk parts from the neck with a slight, sharp snap and has a white, healthy fresh appearance at the juncture of the neck, it indicates premature ripening and the root may be all right. Some growers advise spraying with Bordeaux mixture.

Our experience in this line has been too limited to be of much value, but there is no evidence that the spraying will do any harm. We would certainly recommend trial. It should be done early in the season.

"We wish to reiterate and express our emphatic protest against the bombast and exaggerated statements scattered over the country during the past three years in regard to the wonderful profits in ginseng culture. Actual results are strong enough."

MEDICINAL PROPERTIES

Since many readers desire to know the standing given to ginseng by the medical profession and by the Chinese the following items will be of interest: The St. Louis *Post-Despatch,* of October, 1901, publishes the following information, which was furnished by Mrs. Jeu Hon Yee, the only Chinese woman in St. Louis: "Every good housewife in China keeps ginseng root in the house. It costs a great deal, but it is used in small quantities and an ounce of it lasts a long time. Ginseng tea is a common drink in China. Almost everybody drinks it. It is made by boiling fine cuttings of ginseng in water The tea is good for all sickness, and it keeps disease away. Some of the rich people flavor their meat with ginseng. Only the rich can afford to do this regularly. The root gives the meat a flavor the Chinese people like. Everybody in China is familiar with ginseng. It is the oldest medicine we have. The best ginseng grows in our own woods, and the next best comes from Korea. American ginseng is not so good as either of the other kinds, and sells cheaper. I do not believe the Chinese in the United States use ginseng very much after they come to this country. We do not use it in our own home at all, though we were accustomed to it in China."

The ensuing paragraphs are quoted from Bulletin No. 16 of the Division of Botany already referred to.

"In this country ginseng is considered of little medicinal value. The root is mildly aromatic and slightly stimulant. The Chinese and Koreans, however, place a high value on it, and, indeed, regard it as a panacea. Father Jartoux, while making a map of Tartary under the orders of the Emperor of China, spent some time in Manchuria, where the most valued ginseng grows. The following is his description of the uses to which the Chinese put this root:

" 'They affirm that it is a sovereign remedy for all weaknesses occasioned by excessive fatigues either of body or mind; that it dissolves pituitous humors; that it cures weakness of the lungs and the pleurisy; that it stops vomitings; that it strengthens the stomach and helps the appetite; that it disperses fumes or vapors; that it fortifies the breast, and is a remedy for short and weak breathing; that it strengthens the vital spirits, and increases lymph in the blood; in short, that it is good against dizziness of the head and dimness of sight, and that it prolongs life in old age.'

"Dr. F. P Smith, a medical missionary of recent times, makes the following statement, according to the Chinese materia medica: 'This drug is prepared as an extract, or a decoction, in silver vessels as a rule. Its effects are apparently those of an alterative, tonic, stimulant, carminative, and demulcent nature. It is prescribed in almost every description of disease of a severe character, with few exceptions, but with many reservations as to the stage of the disease in which it may be administered with the greatest benefit and safety. All forms of debility, spermatorrhea, the asthenic hemorrhages, the various forms of severe dyspepsia, the persistent vomiting of pregnant women, malarious affections of a chronic character, the typhoid stages of fever, especially of an epidemic character, are occasions on which the Chinese resort to this drug. Several cases in which life would seem to have been at least prolonged by the taking of doses of this drug, so as to allow of intelligent disposition of property, indicate that some positive efficacy of a sustaining character does really exist in this species of ivywort. The leaves are sold in bundles of the green, fragrant, excellently preserved foliage of the plant. They are said to be emetic and expectorant in their effects.'

"In Korea the cultivated ginseng is smaller than the wild or 'san-sam—literally 'mountain' ginseng—the root of which attains a length of a foot or more and a diameter of an inch and upward. It is said that when this wild root is administered (always at a single dose), the patient loses consciousness for a greater or less time, and for about a month is tortured by boils, eruptions, sleeplessness, and other ills. Rejuvenation then begins, the skin becomes clear, the body healthy, and the person will live, such is the belief, exempt from disease for many years. They think it acts as a preventive by toning up the system.

"Mr. George C. Foulk remarks in Foreign Relations of the United States, 1885:

"'The extreme rarity of san-sam augments the superstitious repute in which it is held; as an intelligent Korean told me, much is said that is only words; nevertheless, he maintained that san-sam was a wonderful medicine in its strengthening effects.'

"It is apparent that the Chinese faith in ginseng rests largely on fanciful grounds, since they prefer roots which, in a measure, resemble the human form. A rude likeness of this kind is frequently discernible, which is said to be increased by manipulation. The name itself signifies 'man plant.' An analogous case is that of the mandrake of the Mediterranean region, long esteemed potent for a similar reason. The root appears to be differently employed according to the source from which it is obtained, probably somewhat on real and somewhat on fictitious grounds. 'The effects of the Manchurian and Korean ginseng are apparently those of an alterative, tonic, stimulant, and carminative nature, while the American and Japanese ginseng are used as demulcent and refrigerant agents.'

"Mr. Horace N. Allen, minister resident and consul-general at Seoul, Korea, writes in United States Consular Reports, No. 53:

"'There is certainly a difference in the effect produced by the use of these two roots [the American and Korean]. The American ginseng is considered by our medical authorities to be "inert." This cannot be said of the Korean root. I have seen the latter produce suppuration in otherwise healthy wounds when surreptitiously given to hasten the slow progress of healing. When the cause was discovered and removed the wounds gradually came into proper condition again. . . .

"'Quinine has been shown to be so much more efficacious in the treatment of the frequent malarial fevers of these countries that ginseng has lost some of its popularity in these cases; but whenever a tonic or a "heating medicine" is needed, ginseng continues to be resorted to, and, by combination with quinine, its reputation will be enhanced rather than diminished.'

"The use of ginseng in different parts of the empire seems to vary considerably. The following statement is made on this point:

"'In the North it is rarely taken except in cases of actual sickness, as the soil and climate are dry and cool, and there is comparatively little malaria. A few of the wealthy people occasionally take an infusion as a precautionary measure during the winter. . . . It is said to be more extensively used by Chinese in the South, owing to the heat and moisture of their soil and climate, being infused with most of their drinks and taken even with some of their solid food as a precautionary measure against sickness.'

"There are stated to be three ways of taking ginseng, viz., as pills, confection, and infusion. Its medicinal value is thought to be diminished by a steaming process to which it is frequently subjected for the improvement of its color. It appears to be given the character of a confection by steeping in honey or by the use of sugar. The wild ginseng of Manchuria is the most highly esteemed, now represented, according to Dr. Smith, by that coming from Shingking. This is and has long been an imperial monopoly.

"A recent consular authority, Mr. I. F. Shephard, presents a classification, the first grade in which is named and described as follows: ' "Imperial ginseng," so called because it is raised or gathered under imperial protection in the parks or hunting grounds, where it is kept free from the profanation of the vulgar herd. This variety ranges from $40 to $200 per pound, and is largely taken up by the wealthy classes in Peking and vicinity, as far as I can learn. It is fine in its appearance, quite in the desired form, and of course very scarce in trade.

" 'Although only an imaginary line divides the Korean peninsula from Manchuria, the ginseng grown in the former place seems to take rank after the Manchurian article. It is said to possess about the same qualities as the Manchurian, and the supposed differences are probably fanciful. Being much cheaper it is more extensively used. The price paid for it ranges from $15 to $35 a pound.

" 'Cultivated ginseng in Korea is a common marketable article, and is produced in large quantities. As in the case of the Manchurian article, its sale has long been a government monopoly, the funds derived from it belonging to the king. But in spite of the death penalty for its private disposal large quantities are smuggled across the Yellow Sea in junks from the western coast of the peninsula to the mainland, and also across the northwestern borders into China, where it always commands a ready market and good price.'

"According to the authority last cited, 'the third grade, called native ginseng, is grown in China near the borders of Korea. This is mostly used to adulterate the Korean article, and is valued at from $1 to $10 per pound.' To this may correspond in some measure a native product noted by Dr. Smith, consisting of the roots of species of Campanula and Adenophora, used as a substitute for ginseng and called by its name.

"Regarding further grades, the above consular authority says:

"'American ginseng is generally regarded as next in classification, but from all I can learn of it I think it belongs rather to the third class, and the last as fourth. When crude it averages about $2 per pound; when clarified, from $4 to $6, and when reclarified, from $6 to $8 per pound. What the clarifying may be I have no absolute information. Some maintain it is only washing and clearing the roots from earth and fibers, and some that it is a process of steeping with honey, which is only done with the best selected specimens.'

"As stated by the same writer, 'The last and poorest quality is the Japanese ginseng, which, like the native product, is used for the adulteration of the Korean supply and other better grades.' Its value is correspondent to that of the native article, i. e., $1 to $10 per pound. According to Dr. Smith, the Japanese ginseng is often adulterated with the roots of *Campanula glauca* and other plants."

Of special interest to American ginseng growers,

at this time, will be the statement that a preparation of ginseng is now being placed upon the American market, and is receiving the attention and endorsement of many reputable physicians who have used it with success in their practice. It appears to act purely as a secernent to the secretory glands of the alimentary canal, thereby materially assisting the proper assimilation of food. In cases characterized by a lack of functional activity in the digestive tract, as well as in general malnutrition, its use has been highly recommended.

PROTECTION BY LAW

As mentioned on Page 13 there are laws protecting ginseng during certain seasons of the year. Since these will be of interest to the grower, especially in the States where these laws are in operation, they are quoted together with the remarks therein contained in Bulletin 16. The reduction of our forest areas and the pasturing of those which remain contribute seriously to the failure of the wild crop. The importance of ginseng is hardly sufficient to have much bearing on the forest question; but, so far as our forests shall be preserved for other reasons, there are two lines along which the law may act toward the preservation of the ginseng supply. The first of these lies in the direction of limiting the time of digging the root. The close season should extend at least from the time the plant starts in the spring until the seed is fully ripe in the fall; for, as we have already seen, ginseng has no means of reproduction except its seed, while at the same time the root is not in good condition during the growing period. It might be wise to make the open season still shorter than this would imply, in order still further to reduce the collection The question may be raised, also, whether the destruction of undergrown roots might not be prohibited, as in the

FIG. 24. A VIEW IN B. L. HART'S PLANTATION AT ROSE HILL, N. Y.

case of small trout and lobsters in some states. If this provision were somewhat difficult to enforce, it would at least call attention to the wastefulness of killing the young plant.

The State of Virginia already has a law limiting the time of collecting, of which the text is as follows:*

AN ACT for the protection of ginseng in the counties of the State.

SEC. 1. *Be it enacted by the general assembly of Virginia,* If any person shall dig any ginseng from the 15th day of March till the 15th day of September, such person, on conviction before a justice of the peace, shall be fined not less than five nor more than ten dollars and costs for each offense.

SEC. 2. *Be it further enacted,* That on the conviction of anyone of such offense the informant shall be entitled to one-half the fine, the remaining half going to the Commonwealth.

SEC. 3. This act shall be in force from its passage.

In the same line, but more stringent, is a law passed by the legislature of Ontario, Canada, in 1891:†

SEC. 1. Except for the purpose of clearing or bringing land into cultivation, no person shall, between the first day of January and the first day of September in any year, cut, root up, gather, or destroy the plant known by the name of ginseng whenever such plant may be found growing in a wild or uncultivated state.

SEC. 2. Any person who contravenes the provision of this act shall, for every such offense, upon summary conviction before any justice of the peace, be subject to a penalty of not less than five dollars or more than twenty dollars, together with costs for

---

*Acts and Joint Resolutions of Virginia, 1875–76, Chapter 90.
†Statutes of the Province of Ontario, 1891, Chapter 52.

prosecution, and one-half of the penalty shall be paid to the prosecutor, unless otherwise ordered by the said justice convicting.

On May 27, 1893, the following amendment to the above law was passed :*

AN ACT to further provide against the extermination of the plant called ginseng.

SEC. 1. Proof of the purchase or sale of ginseng between the first day of January and the first day of September in any year shall be prima facie evidence of a contravention of this act.

SEC. 2. Any person who purchases ginseng, knowing the same to have been cut, rooted up, or gathered between the first day of January and the first day of September, shall be guilty of a contravention of this act.

SEC. 3. In any prosecution under the preceding section proof that the ginseng purchased has been illegally obtained by the vendor shall be prima facie evidence of a contravention of this act by the purchaser.

SEC. 4. This act shall be read as part of the act to prevent the extermination of the plant called ginseng.

From the foregoing it will be seen that the season in Virginia opens half a month later than in Ontario, which is right in view of the difference of latitude. On the other hand, the open season is six months long in Virginia, while in Ontario it is but four months long, and the digging must practically cease with the fall of snow. Considering the comparative mildness of the Virginia winter, a six months' close seems rather short.

A second method of securing protection consists in defending the rights of individual landowners; that

---

*Statutes of the Province of Ontario, 1893, Chapter 43.

is, by prohibiting digging on any land but one's own. The legislature of West Virginia has enacted a law of this purport. It covers the case of other medicinal roots as well as ginseng. The text is as follows:*

SEC. 1. It shall be unlawful for any person to dig ginseng or other medicinal roots, or prospect for the same, on the land of another, in the counties of Pocahontas, Greenbrier, and Webster, without the consent of the owner or owners thereof first had and obtained.

SEC. 2. The provisions of this act shall extend to all the counties of the State: *Provided,* That the county court of any county may, upon the petition of one hundred voters of the county, direct to have the same enforced in their said county or any district or districts thereof.

SEC. 3 Any person violating this act shall be deemed guilty of a misdemeanor, and upon conviction thereof shall be fined not more than fifty dollars, and be confined in the county jail not exceeding two months.

SEC. 4. This act shall be in force from and after the passage thereof.

While a law of this kind does not prevent a man from exterminating ginseng on his own land, it may be assumed that, where the crop is valued, every individual will be prudent enough to husband his own resources. A wanton destruction is most likely to take place on land which is practically public, where no one is sure of anything but what he seizes at once. Nevertheless, in a State having large areas of mountainous and thinly settled territory landowners in many cases either could not or would not care to secure the enforcement of the law; at any rate, would do no more than secure payment for the right of digging, and some further provision would be required. A

---
*Acts of West Virginia, 11th session (1872–73), Chapter 158.

suitable close season might be established to affect at least the lands not guarded by their owners.

Ginseng under cultivation would naturally enjoy the same protection as any other planted crop. Since plantations would generally be made in woodlands, some special provision may be needed, particularly where the digging of the wild plant on the lands of others is not forbidden. The owner of the plantation might be required to post a prohibitory notice.

Other States than those mentioned do not appear to have legislated in behalf of ginseng.

INDEX.

	Page
Advancing price	47
Advantages of growing ginseng	50
Advice to would-be growers	50
Age and seed bearing	73
Age and size	116, 127
Age and quality	127
Age and weight	73, 110
Aged specimens	10
American ginseng, demand for	105
American ginseng discovered	3
American ginseng in Asia	96, 105
American ginseng trade started	3
Annual development of the plant	8
Annual growth of roots	12
Annual setting of seed	18
Appearance of plants	6, 7, 9
Appearance of seedlings	6
Apple trees, beds under	25
Artificial propagation	30, 65, 121
Ashes	33, 115, 116, 117
Attacks of mice	27
Autumn transplanting	15, 59
Beds, level	20
Beds, orchard	23
Beds, preparation of permanent 50, 61, 117, 118, 124	
Beds, treatment of	30
Beds under apple trees	25
Beds under cherry trees	25
Beds unnecessary	21
Beginning	14
Berries	9
Berries fail to set	56
Berries first ripe	57
Berries, gathering	57
Best season to dig	11
Blossoms, pinching	57, 127
Blossoms, sterile	55
Bordeaux mixture	68, 69, 129
Boring beetles	45
Botany of the plant	5, 14
Broken roots	95
Brush covering	28, 117, 123
Bud at the root crown	16
Burning of Korean ginseng	104
Canadian ginseng	77
Capacity of dryer	43
Carbon bisulphide	46
Cattle and sheep	31
Cellar storage and seed	17
Change of soil	61, 125
Cherry trees, beds under	25
Chickens in beds	37
Chinese ginseng, cultivated	109
Clarification	75
Clarified root in market	12
Cleaning	42

	Page
Cleanliness of package of roots	46, 74
Climate	18
Climate, change of	57
Collectors' profits decreasing	48
Consul Allen's letter	95, 104
Consul Allen quoted	133
Consul Ragsdale's letter	105
Consul Rubles's letter	99
Consul Wildman's letter	94, 96
Covers	62
Crash of prices	86
Cricket, ginseng	67
Crosley's letter, Messrs	110
Crown roots, new	10
Cultivated root in China	101
Cultivated root in the market	71
Cultivated vs. wild root 70, 72, 73, 78, 85, 121	
Cultivation	28
Dealers in Asia	99, 102
Dealers' prices	47
Demand	50
Demand and supply	81, 82, 84, 85
Depth of planting	117
Destroying beetles	46
Destruction of Korean ginseng	104
Development, annual	8
Dibble	64, 117
Digger	60
Digging	41, 42
Digging wild plants	16
Discovery of American ginseng	3
Diseases	67, 126, 129
Distance between plants	30, 62, 115, 123
Distance to plant seed	27
Divisible root	12
Drainage	20, 61, 125
Dryer, capacity of	43
Dryer, cost of	43
Dryer, homemade	42, 43
Dryer, operating	44
Drying	42
Drying, loss of weight in	72, 110
Drying of seed in summer	17
Duties on ginseng	95
Early maturing variety	39
Early trade ruined	6
Eisenbauer's letter	81
Enemies	36, 66
Enriching the soil	65
Estimates	87, 91, 92, 93
Exaggeration	90
Export decreasing	47
Export direct	97
Export from Canada	77
Exports statistics	47, 79
Exposures	19

INDEX.

	Page
Flavor of cultivated root	73, 79, 80, 81
Flowers, pinching	57, 127
Flowers, sterile	65
Fly white	67
Foulk, George C., quoted	106, 132
Fraser's letter, Mr	116
Freezing, danger of	15
Freezing of seeds	17
Freezing of stored roots	15
Fruit fails to set	15
Germination first spring	59, 69, 123
Ginseng, advantages of growing	50
Ginseng, American discovered	3
Ginseng, American trade started	3
Ginseng digger	60
Ginseng in Canada	77
Ginseng, reproduction	12
Ginseng, uses of	2
Grading for market	46, 97, 98, 101, 102, 105, 106, 127, 134
Ground bone	32
Growers, organization of	71
Hardiness	129
Hard pan	125
Hart's letter, Mr	110
Hartzel & Co's clarifying method	76
History	1, 5
Hong Kong distributing center	100
Hoe for digging	60
Horse for weeding	26
Humus	61, 114, 116, 125
Humus, decay of	66
Iida's letter	103
Improvement of stock	37
Industry, promising	50
Influence of "sang-diggers"	13
Injured roots	29
Inspection in market	97, 98
Insects	36
Japanese ginseng	83, 87, 88, 89, 106, 125
Kelsey's lath shade	62
Kelsey's planting board	63
Kirin ginseng	105
Korean crop, 1901	104
Korean cultivated ginseng	107
Korean ginseng	96, 101
Korean ginseng market	102
Korean root in Hong Kong	101, 103, 105
Large seed quick germinating	39
Leaf mulch	28
Level beds	20
Lime for slugs	66
Location	18
Male flowers	55
Manchurian ginseng	134
Manure, avoid fresh	32
Manuring	32, 65, 113, 117
Marker for setting seed	37, 63
Market	74, 81, 97
Market, overstocked	83, 85
Market requirements	102
Maturity	111, 116
Mice	17, 36, 66, 67, 124
Misrepresentation	90
Moisture-holding power of soil	20
Moles	36, 37, 66
Muck	61
Mulch, leaf	28
Mulches	32
Mulch, muck	28
Mutilated roots	41
Natural home	14
Nematodes	66, 126
Nitrate of soda	66, 117
Nitrogenous fertilizer	65

	Page
Northern exposures best	19
Northern vs southern stock	57, 58
Nub	95
Nub in ginseng	128
Nusbaum's letter, Mr	113
Open ground storage of seed	17
Orchard beds	23
Organization	71
Oven drying	42
Packing	95, 97, 102
Parent's letter, Mr	111
Payson's letter, Mr	121
Peanut ginseng	128
Phosphates	32
Pike's letter, Mr	109
Pistillate flowers	55
Planting board	27, 63, 115, 117
Plants, annual development	8
Potash	32
Preparation for market	41
Preparation of beds	21, 25
Preparation of permanent beds	25
Prices advancing	47
Prices and seed	73, 87, 92, 120
Prices, fall of	86, 93
Prices for series of years	47, 79, 80, 81, 82
Prices in Asia	94, 95
Prices of 1898	43
Prices of 1891	79, 80, 81, 82
Prices paid by leaders	47
Profits	46, 87
Propagation, artificial	30, 65, 121
Protection of beds	120, 136
Purchaser must see goods	97
Quality	127
Raised beds	23
Root decay	36
Root, divisible	12
Roots, annual growth of	12
Roots, broken	95
Roots, cleaning	42
Roots, first class	40
Roots, four years old	12
Roots, freezing of stored	15
Roots from cuttings	13
Roots, keeping dried	46
Roots, kind preferred	41
Roots, new crown	10
Roots, old	10
Roots, storing dry	45
Roots, trimming dry	44
Roots, undersized	41
Root vs seed	127
Rotation of crops	61, 125
Rotting of seed	18
Samples	94, 97
Sample shipment	97
Seed and high prices	73
Seed, annual setting	18
Seed-bearing and age	73
Seed beds	21
Seed, danger of drying of	16
Seeding, annual	18
Seedlings, appearance of	5
Seedlings, time of appearance	5
Seed planting	26
Seed ripens	116
Seed, storage in cellar	17
Seed stratifying	17, 59
Seed vs. roots	127
Seed, yield of	91, 110, 123, 125
Selection for improvement	69, 70
Shade and soil	61
Shade, climbing perennial	33
Shade, forest	33

INDEX.

	Page		Page
Shade, lath	34, 62, 107, 113, 118	Succession of crops	61, 125
Shade, low lath	36	Sun drying	42
Shade, planting annual	23	Superstitions	42
Shades	33	Supply and demand	81, 82, 84, 85
Shade, storing lath	35	Texture of soil for older plants	26
Shade, vertical	36	Thieves	31, 67
Shipment, direct	97	Three-year-old root	11
Shipments not uniform	98	Time not to dig	13
Shipping	46	Time plants appear	5
Sifting seed	18	Time seedlings appear	28
Size and age	116, 127	Time to dig	14
Size of nursery bed	23	Time to mature	30
Sloping beds	20	Time to transplant	15
Slugs	66	Trade started in American ginseng	3
Smith quoted, Dr	131	Transplanting	63
Smuggling	96	Transplanting, time for	15
Snails	36, 66	Treatment for permanent beds	30
Soil	19, 21, 59, 60, 113, 116, 125	Tree roots	23
Soil and shade	51	Trimming roots	29
Soil, avoid poor	33	Trowel for digging	16
Soil, change of	25, 61	Trowel for setting	30
Southern plants in the North	57, 58, 123, 128	Undersized roots	41
Southern exposures poorest	19	Uses of ginseng	2
Sowing at once	18	Variety, new	70
Space needed for ounce of seed	23	Walks, width of	25
Spade for digging	16	Wallace Bros.' prices	80
Speyer & Sons' prices	81	Washing	42
Spraying	68, 129	Water test	59
Spring-set plants	16, 118	Weeding	26, 29
Sprouting first spring	59, 69, 123	Weeding horse	26
Staminate flowers	65	Weight after drying	72, 110
Stanton's letter, Mr	49, 125	Weight and age	73, 110
Statistics of export	47	Wells & Co.'s letter	82
Storing	15	Width of beds	23
Storing the seed	17	Wild root vs. cultivated	40, 79, 85, 121
Stove drying	42	Wild supply declining	78
Stratifying seed	59, 123	Wilting	129
		Wood ashes	33

ADVERTISEMENTS.

HEADQUARTERS FOR GINSENG

Samuel Wells & Co.
Exporters

Cincinnati, Ohio

Highest Market Prices
Prompt Returns

....Ginseng

We are very extensive buyers of this article, and parties who send us their root may be assured of receiving its full market value and a prompt remittance.

Write us for price list.

BELT, BUTLER CO.
83 Spring St., NEW YORK

Farm   Fruits
Garden   Flowers   Dogs
Cattle   Swine
Sheep   Horses
Pet-Stock
Boating   Fishing   Bees
Hunting
Shooting   Architecture

Free Catalogue of the largest line of Rural Books in the country to all applying

<u>Address</u> **Orange Judd Company** New York, N Y
Chicago, Ill

ADVERTISEMENTS.

Wm. Eisenhauer & Co.

378-380 West Broadway, New York

Buyers
and Exporters of

GINSENG

Highest prices paid for Ginseng from
all sections at all times

Returns sent immediately and payment
made by check, money-order,
or in any other way you may prefer

Write for Prices

Correspondence and shipments
solicited

References Furnished

ADVERTISEMENTS.

Headquarters in America for
Ginseng Seeds and Plants
and at fair prices

An illustrated circular giving concise instructions for successfully cultivating this valuable root for 10 cents.

PRICE LIST FREE

Parties who contemplate Ginseng culture on an extensive scale will do well to correspond with us before placing an order. We give special terms and detailed advice. It pays us to make our customers successful growers. We have eighteen years' experience in growing all kinds of Hardy Native Plants (A unique descriptive catalogue of American Native Plants filled with original half tone illustrations free, if you are interested.) Remember we are **Ginseng specialists.**

Address

HARLAN P. KELSEY

Tremont Building, Boston, Mass.

Proprietor Highlands Nursery, 3800 feet elevation in the Carolina mountains. 65 acres.

The Great Agricultural Weeklies

American Agriculturist, 52 Lafayette Place, New York
For the Middle States, Ohio and the South

New England Homestead, Springfield, Mass.
For the Eastern States.

Orange Judd Farmer, Marquette Building, Chicago, Ill.
For the Western, Central, South-Western and Pacific States.

Cover every feature of rural economy, best market reports, valuable household and family departments.

Send for specimen copies of the one for your section.

Subscription Price **$1.00** per year, postpaid

Liberal premium offers.

ORANGE JUDD COMPANY, Publishers

New York   Chicago   Springfield, Mass.